# STREET FOOD VIETNAM

JERRY MAI

Photography by Chris Middleton

Smith Street Books

INTRODUCTION 08
THE VIETNAMESE PANTRY 14


SNACKS 20
RICE PAPER 38
BANH MI 60
GRILL 74
BIA HOI 94
SALADS 108
NOODLE SOUPS 130
OFFICE RICE 160
DESSERTS 180
BASICS 202


ACKNOWLEDGEMENTS 216
ABOUT THE AUTHOR 218
INDEX 219

INTRODUCTION

I was born in Vietnam in the late 1970s, but in 1984 my family moved to Australia and I didn't return to the country of my birth until 1992. I was 15 at the time, and the trip was completely overwhelming: the incredible smells, flavours, people and, of course, the crazy traffic! It was my first introduction to Vietnamese street food, and I was immediately hooked. The streets were filled with food vendors selling endless dishes, some of which I'd never seen before. The smell of the smoke and meat cooking on those little charcoal grills lured me to the stalls and had me eagerly watching what was being cooked up.

The streets may have changed and modernised over the last 25 years, but many of the local street-food dishes have stood the test of time (along with a few flash-in-the-pans that have come and gone). Every year I visit different regions of Vietnam to try new food experiences, and I am never disappointed. As a chef, I find myself reinvigorated after each visit and inspired to recreate the flavours I discover on my journeys in new and unique ways.

This book is the culmination of my long love affair with Vietnamese food. It encapsulates the dishes that I dream of when I'm not in Vietnam, along with the food I love to make in my restaurants. Vietnamese food is the heart and soul of what I cook, and it's a big part of what I love about my heritage.

Some of the recipes in this book are dishes I grew up eating at home. As a child, I would stand on a stool in the kitchen and watch my mum slave over the stove, whipping up amazing food for our family and friends to enjoy. If banh xeo was for dinner, the house would be filled with the smell of fresh herbs and the sound of sizzling as the batter hit the hot wok. Banh xeo night at home was like playing musical chairs, as each person took turns to make the next pancake. I loved the hands-on nature of the dish and the challenge between me and my brothers to see who would make the best banh xeo!

Today, when I walk into my mum's house and smell the aroma of pho simmering slowly on the stove, it fills me with so many happy childhood memories, along with the knowledge of how much love she has put into it. Even now, my brothers and I can hardly wait for the broth to be ready, so we can slurp down a bowl! On these occasions, word inevitably gets out that Mum is making a big pot of her famous pho and soon other family members and friends arrive. We gather around the dining table catching up and chatting, all while waiting to dig in.

My mother's signature dish, however, would have to be hu tieu nam vang, a dish she learned to make in Phnom Penh after the Cambodian Civil War, and where she later opened a restaurant specialising in this noodle soup. To me, my mum's hu tieu nam vang is still the best, and you will find the recipe on page 137.

Unsurprisingly, my mother is the main inspiration for my lifelong love of cooking. I see the food that I cook and my restaurant dining room as an extension of my family dining room. It's where I get to share my culture and the dishes I grew up with and love. My obsession with street food is what inspired me to open my first food venue, Pho Nom. From there I started looking to Vietnam's neighbouring countries to expand my understanding and knowledge of Southeast Asian cuisine. This led me to open my restaurant Annam, which not only celebrates Vietnamese food, but also the amazing culinary diversity of the whole region.

Food memories are often the most intense: they bring us back to our childhoods and to our mothers' and grandmothers' laps; they encourage us to travel to find the dishes or experiences we lovingly recall; and they lure us back to unique places captured in time. *Street Food Vietnam* is filled with my food memories, but hopefully through cooking the recipes in this book, they will reignite or create new memories for you, too. Enjoy!

# THE VIETNAMESE PANTRY

Here are the basic ingredients and equipment that you'll find in every Vietnamese kitchen – staples that feature in many of the recipes in this book. You can find most of these goods at your local Asian supermarket.

**Anchovy sauce (mắm nêm)**
Mam nem is fermented salted anchovies. It is very strong in taste and smell, and is normally diluted when used to make the sauce of the same name.

**Banana blossom (bắp chuối)**
Also known as banana flower, banana blossom is the edible flower of the banana plant. The outer leaves are discarded and the inner 'hearts' are sliced and used in salads.

**Cassia bark (quế)**
Similar to cinnamon, this spice is used to add a deep, earthy tone to soups and heavy braises.

**Fish sauce (nước mắm)**
Fish sauce is the essence of Vietnamese food. It is made by fermenting anchovies and sea salt for 12–14 months. In Vietnamese cooking, a good fish sauce is as important as a good olive oil. When buying fish sauce, look for good-quality brands, such as Dũ Sơn or Red Boat. The regions that produce the best nuoc mam in Vietnam are Phú Quốc and Phan Thiết. Nuoc mam nhi is the first press (the equivalent of extra-virgin olive oil) and is reserved for dipping sauces and salads. The second press is less expensive and is used for cooking. When purchasing your nuoc mam, look for the region it comes from and if it's the first press.

**Glass noodles (miến)**
Also called cellophane noodles, these thin, transparent noodles are used in soups or as an addition to mince (ground) meat for stuffing.

**Green mango (xoài xanh)**
Tart, crisp and refreshing with an underlying mango flavour, green mango is used in salads and eaten with salt and pounded chilli as a snack.

**Green papaya (đu đủ xanh)**
Green papaya is simply the unripe papaya fruit. When choosing green papaya, make sure it is green, firm and the flesh is white with no traces of orange.

**Hoi sin sauce (sốt tương ngọt)**
A thick, sweet Chinese barbecue sauce made from salted black beans, onions and garlic. In Vietnamese cooking, hoi sin sauce is mainly used as a table condiment and as a flavouring for meat, poultry and shellfish dishes.

**Master stock (cổ phiếu chính)**
This is a stock that has been kept 'alive' for a great length of time by being topped up and added to every time it is used. It has so many uses: from making broths and poaching, to braising meat and poultry. Master stock is made from chicken stock, light soy sauce, dark soy sauce, rock sugar, cassia bark, star anise, orange peel and shao xing wine.

### Morning glory (rau muống)

Also known as water spinach, morning glory is a green vegetable that's usually stir-fried or used as a table herb in Vietnamese cooking. The Vietnamese often use a 'morning glory shredder' to cut the stems into strands. This simple but genius piece of equipment is essentially a 20 cm–30 cm (8 in– 12 in) metal rod, which is pointy at one end and has a round plastic top with internal blades at the other. To use, thread a stem of morning glory onto the rod and push it through the blade at the top. The blade shreds the stem into thin curls – easy!

### Oyster sauce (sốt hàu)

This sauce is an extract from oysters mixed with sugar and salt and thickened with cornflour (corn starch). It's a great addition to stir-fries.

### Rice flour (bột gạo)

Rice flour is simply flour milled from rice. In Vietnamese cooking it is generally used in batters and to coat ingredients before deep-frying. It is an excellent gluten-free substitute for wheat flour.

### Rice noodles (bún)

A staple in Vietnamese cooking, rice noodles are widely used in soups, rice paper rolls and salads. There are several varieties, ranging from thin to thick, which are used in different dishes. When choosing noodles, make sure you select the correct type of noodle for the dish.

### Rice paper (bánh tráng)

Rice paper is a staple in Vietnamese food. Once rehydrated, it becomes soft and silky and is commonly used as a wrapper for herbs, salad and bun (rice noodles). Rice paper can also be fried until crisp and eaten like a cracker. A fairly new food trend also sees the rice paper cut up and tossed in salads.

### Shrimp sauce (mắm ruốc)

Shrimp sauce is widely used as a dipping sauce or marinade in northern Vietnamese cuisine. It is made from mashed marinated shrimp, which is then fermented for a long time in bottles.

### Star anise (cánh hồi)

This six-to-eight pointed spice imparts a flavour resembling cinnamon and cloves. It is used to flavour soups and stews, as well as marinades. It is an essential ingredient in pho.

### Thin egg noodles (mì trứng)

These noodles are a legacy of Chinese occupation in Vietnam. They are commonly used in soups and stir-fries.

# Herbs

No Vietnamese dish is complete without some fragrant herbs! Fresh herbs bring vibrancy to dishes, as well as being key ingredients in salads and as an accompaniment to soups and pancakes.

### Betel leaf (lá lốt)
Betel leaves have bitter characteristics with sweet aromatics. In Vietnamese cooking they can be wrapped around minced (ground) beef and grilled, used in stir-fries or eaten raw. They also have medicinal purposes – the juice of the betel leaf mixed with honey serves as a good tonic, and when the leaves are soaked in mustard oil and warmed, they can be applied to the chest area to relieve coughs and difficulties in breathing. The leaves are also used as an antiseptic.

### Elephant ear stalk (bạc hà)
Long, spongy stalks great for adding to rice paper rolls.

### Mint (húng lủi)
With large, oval leaves and a sweet, fresh taste, regular mint is used in salads and herb plates on the table.

### Rice paddy herb (ngò om)
This herb with small oval leaves has a citrus and mild cumin flavour. It's perfect in certain soups and salads.

### Sawtooth coriander (ngò gai)
Long, narrow serrated leaves with a strong coriander flavour. Perfect in pho and other soups.

### Shiso (tía tô)
Peppery in flavour with large leaves that are purple on one side and dark green on the other. Shiso is normally used in salads, as a herb on the table for soups or wrapped in rice paper rolls.

### Thai basil (rau quế)
Best eaten with pho, Thai basil has a sweet aniseed flavour with notes of cinnamon.

### Vietnamese mint (rau răm)
Spicy and peppery, Vietnamese mint can be identified by its long, narrow leaves. It's frequently used in salads and beef dishes.

# Kitchen equipment

The majority of Vietnamese dishes can be made using just a few basic items of kitchen equipment. Below are everyday utensils found in every Vietnamese kitchen.

### Bamboo steamer
An essential item used for steaming meats, cakes and desserts. It locks in flavour and keeps the food moist.

### Cleaver
A heavy-based knife used to chop through bones and larger pieces of meat. Lighter cleavers are used for delicate vegetable cutting.

### Kitchen scissors
Vietnamese home cooks use scissors more than a knife to cut herbs, vegetables, chicken and fish. They are easier to use, and ideal when space is limited – such as in Vietnamese kitchens – as you don't need as much space to set up a chopping board.

### Mortar and pestle
Used for grinding spices and to pound lemongrass, chilli and garlic for sauces. Pounding the ingredients gives a rounded flavour and smoother texture.

### Wok
An essential pan used to stir-fry over rapid heat to seal in flavour.

Snacks make up a large part of how Vietnamese people eat – we like to graze on various foods throughout the day, and the best way to snack in Vietnam is to head outside and see what the local street-food stalls have on offer. There are many vendors who roam the streets selling their specialties, and one of the great things about eating in Vietnam is that no two stalls are the same when it comes to food. Snacks might include crispy pancakes, bun (rice noodles), fritters, sweet cakes and green or unripe fruit, such as mango, starfruit and guava, along with many more delicious bites to see you through from breakfast to lunch and from lunch to dinner.

# BÁNH KHỌT

Savoury mini coconut pancakes

Banh khot is a great little snack that's crispy on the outside and rich and creamy on the inside. I don't make these at home very often, and I'm not sure why as they are so easy to make. I look forward to eating them every year during the Tết festival (Vietnamese New Year) street parties, where the atmosphere always reminds me of Vietnam.

425 g (15 oz/2½ cups) rice flour
1 teaspoon ground turmeric
250 ml (8½ fl oz/1 cup) coconut cream
1 teaspoon sea salt
1 tablespoon vegetable oil, plus extra
    for greasing and frying
25–30 small green prawns (shrimp), peeled
    and deveined

**To serve**
3 tablespoons Prawn floss (see page 213)
Pickled carrot and daikon (see page 209)
thinly sliced bird's eye chillies
125 ml (4 fl oz/½ cup) Nuoc mam dipping sauce
    (see page 206)

**1**  Combine the rice flour, turmeric, coconut cream, salt and 600 ml (20½ fl oz) water in a bowl. Add the oil and mix well, making sure there are no lumps in the batter. Set aside to rest for at least 2 hours.

**2**  Give the rested batter a good stir to get it ready to use.

**3**  Place a 12-hole banh khot pan (see note) over medium heat and generously grease the holes. Working quickly so the banh khot cook at the same time, evenly spoon the batter into the holes until filled to the top. Top each of the banh khot with a prawn, then cover and cook for 1 minute.

**4**  Remove the lid and drizzle a little oil down the side of each banh khot to help them crisp up and come away easily from the pan. The more oil you use, the crispier they will be. Continue to cook the banh khot for 7–10 minutes, until the batter has turned a wonderful yellow colour. Using a spoon, carefully remove the pancakes from the pan and transfer to a plate. Top with ½ teaspoon prawn floss, a few pickles and sliced chillies.

**5**  Serve immediately with the nuoc mam for drizzling over and dipping (these are best eaten straight away), then continue to make batches of banh khot with the remaining ingredients until you've used everything up.

**Note:** Banh khot pans can be bought online or at most Asian kitchenware stores. Alternatively, a Dutch pancake pan would suffice, but I have also seen banh khot cooked in muffins tins by very enterprising cooks.

# BÁNH XÈO

Crispy Vietnamese pancakes

Serves 4

The name banh xeo comes from the sound of the batter hitting the hot frying pan (xeo means sizzle). I absolutely love these crispy pancakes with their accompanying fragrant, fresh herbs. I like to wrap mouthfuls of banh xeo and herbs in lettuce leaves, whereas my mum prefers to use mustard leaves. I roll it up as best as I can and dip it in the nuoc mam – if I get too excited with the nuoc mam, it dribbles down my arm! Oh, and only rookies pour the nuoc mam in the wrap. Be a true Vietnamese and dip instead!

340 g (12 oz) rice flour
125 ml (4 fl oz/½ cup) coconut milk
2 teaspoons ground turmeric
2 tablespoons vegetable oil, plus extra
   for drizzling
1 teaspoon sea salt
1 egg
500 g (1 lb 2 oz) pork belly
16 small green prawns (shrimp), peeled,
   deveined and halved lengthways
500 g (1 lb 2 oz) bean sprouts

**To serve**
lettuce leaves or mustard leaves
1 bunch Vietnamese mint
1 bunch mint
1 bunch shiso
Nuoc mam dipping sauce (see page 206)

**1**   Whisk the flour, coconut milk, turmeric, oil, salt, egg and 600 ml (20½ fl oz) water in a bowl. Set aside to rest for 3 hours.

**2**   Bring a large saucepan of water to the boil and add a pinch of salt. Add the pork belly, then reduce the heat to a simmer and cook for 40 minutes. Drain and set aside to cool, then cut into thin slices.

**3**   Heat a medium non-stick frying pan over medium-high heat, add 5–6 slices of the pork belly and stir-fry for 2–3 minutes until lightly golden. Pour about 60 ml (2 fl oz/¼ cup) of the batter into the pan and swirl to cover the base of the pan and the pork belly (tip any excess batter back into the bowl – the thinner the pancake the crispier it will be). Cook for 5–7 minutes, until the base of the pancake is golden brown, then drizzle a little oil down the inside of the pan (this helps the pancake to get even more crispy). Scatter four prawn halves and a handful of bean sprouts over one half of the pancake and fold the other half over the top. Cook for a further 2 minutes, then remove from the pan, transfer to a serving plate and take to the table (these are best eaten straight away).

**4**   Pile the lettuce or mustard leaves and herbs onto a serving plate and place in the middle of the table for everyone to help themselves. Invite guests to tear off some of the pancake, place in a lettuce leaf and top with a few herbs. Roll up tightly and dip in the nuoc mam.

**5**   Repeat with the remaining pancake ingredients to make eight banh xeo.

# BÁNH CUỐN CUA
Crab in silken rice noodle rolls

Banh cuon is traditionally eaten at breakfast but can also be enjoyed throughout the day. This version is a little more luxurious than the traditional breakfast option usually found in Vietnam.

You need to start this recipe the day before to allow the batter to completely rest.

———

200 g (7 oz) rice flour
60 g (2 oz) glutinous rice flour
1 tablespoon vegetable oil, plus extra
  for shallow-frying and brushing
pinch of sea salt

**Filling**
2 tablespoons vegetable oil
1 teaspoon minced ginger
2 garlic cloves, minced
1 whole leek, sliced into half moons
1 tablespoon white soy sauce or light soy sauce
1 teaspoon kombu extract powder (see note)
  or 1 pinch of sea salt
500 g (1 lb 2 oz) fresh spanner crab meat or any
  good-quality fresh crab meat

**To serve**
2 bird's eye chillies, thinly sliced
Fried shallots (see page 212)
Nuoc mam dipping sauce (see page 206)
180 g (6½ oz/2 cups) blanched bean sprouts
1 bunch mint
1 bunch Thai basil

**1**  Combine the rice flours, oil, salt and 600 ml (20½ fl oz) water in a large bowl and mix well. Set aside to rest overnight.

**2**  To make the filling, heat the oil in a wok or large frying pan over medium–high heat. Add the ginger, garlic and leek and stir-fry for 2–3 minutes, until fragrant and soft. Season with the white soy and kombu extract, then add the crab meat and cook for a further 3 minutes, stirring to combine. Remove from the heat and set aside to cool.

**3**  Heat 1 teaspoon of oil in a 15 cm (6 in) frying pan with a lid over low heat and pour in 3 tablespoons of the batter. Swirl to cover the base of the pan, then cover and cook for 3–5 minutes until cooked through. Flip the rice sheet onto a plate lightly brushed with oil, top with a little of the crab mixture and roll into a log. (It usually takes me a few goes to get these right; persevere as it does get easier with practice).

**4**  Repeat with the remaining batter and filling to make 20 crab rolls.

**5**  Place the filled banh cuon on plates and top with a little sliced chilli, some fried shallots and a drizzle of nuoc mam. Serve with the bean sprouts, mint and Thai basil on the side.

**Note:** Kombu extract powder can be purchased from Japanese grocers.

# BÁNH TÔM

School prawn and sweet potato fritters

I first ate these prawn fritters in Hanoi by the West Lake, bought from a little lady frying them by the water. The smell of the fried prawns drew me in, so I plonked myself next to her on a stool way too small for my arse (this happens to me a lot in Vietnam – I wish they made larger plastic furniture!). I ate so many fritters that day, and I've never forgotten the taste. This recipe is my interpretation of the dish.

---

2 litres (2 qts) vegetable oil, for deep-frying
500 g (1 lb 2 oz) sweet potato, peeled and cut
    into matchsticks
200 g (7 oz) whole school prawns (small shrimp)

**Batter**
200 g (7 oz) rice flour
200 g (7 oz) glutinous rice flour
200 g (7 oz) tapioca flour

**To serve**
1 iceberg lettuce, leaves separated
1 bunch Vietnamese mint, leaves picked
1 bunch shiso, leaves picked
Nuoc mam dipping sauce (see page 206)

**1** Whisk the batter ingredients and 250 ml (8½ fl oz/1 cup) water in a large bowl, making sure there are no lumps.

**2** Heat the oil in a large saucepan over medium–high heat until it reaches 180°C (350°F) on a kitchen thermometer.

**3** Add the sweet potato and prawns to the batter and toss well to coat. In the bowl, loosely divide the mixture into eight portions. Carefully spoon four portions of the fritter mixture into the oil and cook, turning occasionally, for 8–10 minutes, until golden and crispy. Use a slotted spoon to remove the fritters from the oil and drain on a plate lined with paper towel. Repeat with the remaining portions of batter.

**4** Serve the fritters either on a large serving platter or on individual plates with the lettuce leaves, Vietnamese mint, shiso and nuoc mam on the side. Wrap the fritters and a few herbs in the lettuce cups, then dip into the nuoc mam. Enjoy!

# BÁNH BÈO

Waterfern cakes

Whenever I'm in Saigon, my first stop is always a small stall in Ben Thanh Market that sells amazing banh beo. The owner never smiles but serves the banh beo while her staff run around clearing and serving customers. One plate is never enough, and I always end up ordering another. One day I will get her to crack a smile at me!

You need to start this recipe the day before.

100 g (3½ oz/½ cup) split mung beans (mung dal)
200 g (7 oz) pork fat, diced into large cubes
vegetable oil, for greasing
3 tablespoons Prawn floss (see page 213)
80 ml (2½ fl oz/⅓ cup) Spring onion oil (see page 207)
Nuoc mam dipping sauce (see page 206), for drizzling
    and dipping

**Batter**
340 g (12 oz/2 cups) rice flour
2 tablespoons tapioca flour
1 teaspoon salt
2 teaspoons vegetable oil

**1** Place the mung beans in a large bowl and cover with cold water. Set aside to soak overnight.

**2** Make the batter by whisking the ingredients and 1 litre (34 fl oz/4 cups) water in a large bowl. Set aside to rest for 2 hours.

**3** Meanwhile, drain the mung beans, transfer to a saucepan and cover with water. Simmer over medium–low heat for 10–15 minutes until soft. Drain the beans and process in a blender until smooth.

**4** Place the pork fat in a frying pan over high heat. Render the fat on all sides for 15–20 minutes until crispy, then transfer to a plate lined with paper towel to drain.

**5** I normally use small shallow dipping bowls to cook my banh beo. First, brush the dipping bowls with a little oil (this will make it easier to remove the banh beo once they are cooked). Working in batches, arrange the bowls in the base of a large bamboo steamer and fill each bowl with 2 tablespoons of the batter – you only want a thin layer. Set the steamer over a saucepan of simmering water and steam for 10 minutes or until the cakes are set. Carefully remove the cakes from the dipping bowls and repeat with the remaining batter.

**6** To serve, spoon a little mung bean paste onto the cakes and top with 3–4 pieces of pork fat and the prawn floss. Drizzle the spring onion oil and a little of the nuoc mam over the banh beo, and serve with more nuoc mam on the side for dipping.

FISH SAUCE

Fish sauce is the essence of Vietnamese cooking. It features in pretty much every dish and is used in place of salt to season foods.

The process of making fish sauce is relatively simple. Anchovies and salt are layered in ceramic or wooden barrels and left to ferment. After 12 months, the barrels are emptied releasing the 'first press' fish sauce – similar to the first press of olive oil – which is the most sought-after and valued liquid. The first press is amber in colour, aromatic and salty with a hint of sweetness. The barrels are then stored for a further 6–12 months, which produces the second press fish sauce, which is saltier and stronger in flavour.

Some of the best fish sauces in Vietnam come from Phú Quốc and Phan Thiết. Both are coastal towns with large fishing fleets that catch the precious anchovies needed to make the sauce. Lesser-quality brands of fish sauce use a mixture of fish instead of just anchovies, and these inferior options are simply not as good. Another factor leading to diminished quality of fish sauce is the level of nitrogen in the sauce – the more nitrogen present, the higher the grade of sauce. Nitrogen levels are marked next to an 'N' on the bottle and good-quality fish sauce will always carry this label.

At my restaurants Pho Nom and Annam, I use Dũ Sơn fish sauce from Phú Quốc, which is aromatic without being too pungent and has a lovely saltiness with a hint of sweetness on the back palate. It's versatile enough to use on its own as a dipping sauce or with other ingredients.

RICE RICE
RICE RICE
RICE RICE
RICE RICE

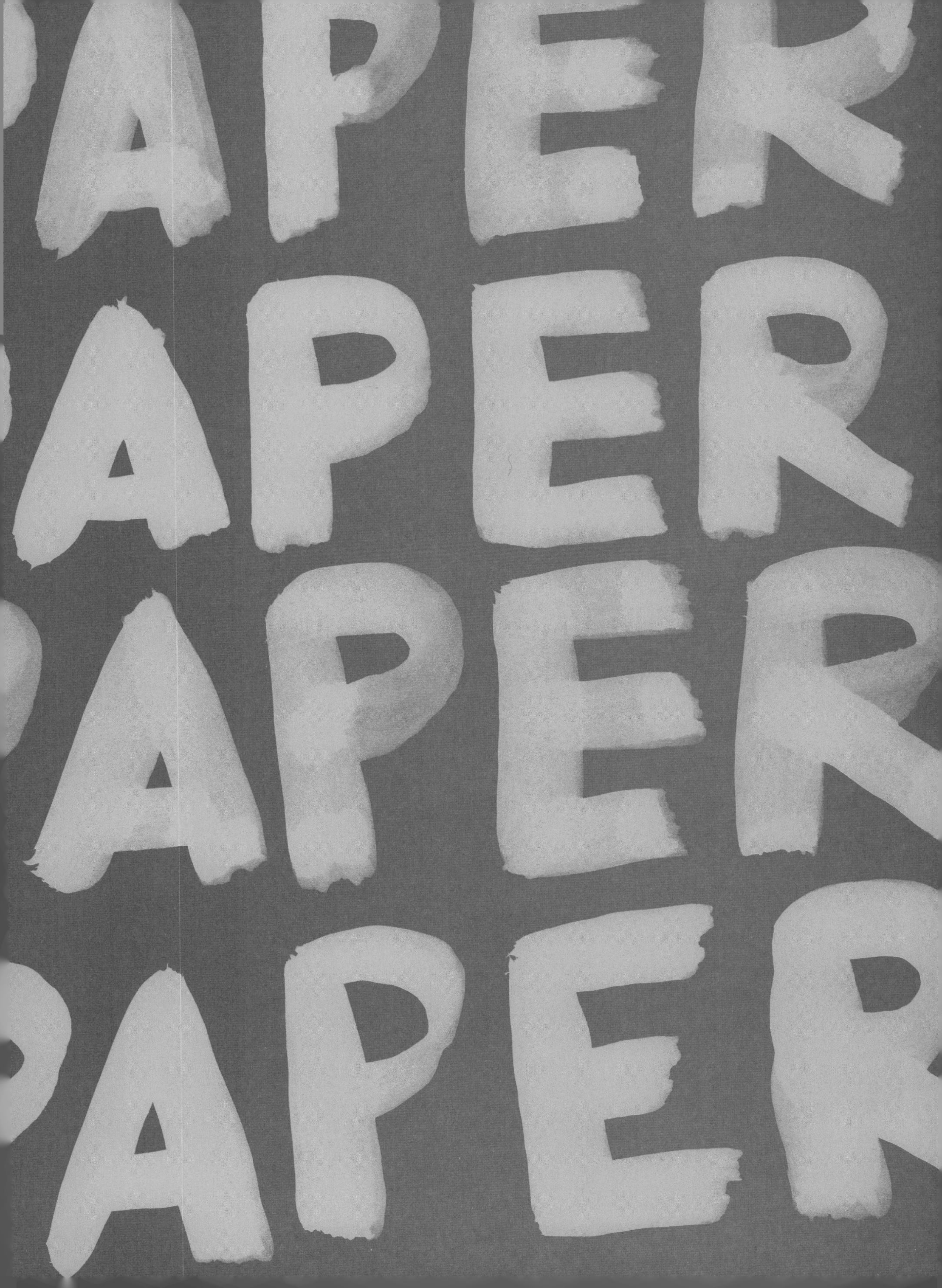
APER
APER
APER
APER

Rice paper forms the base of many Vietnamese dishes. It is used to wrap ingredients and carry flavour and texture: from the rice paper rolls that we all know and love, to accompanying salad plates placed in the centre of the table to wrap herbs, meat and fish.

The rice paper you find in Vietnamese markets is the result of a long, tedious, handmade process. First, the rice is ground to make a flour, which is then transformed into a batter. A thin layer of this batter is then spread over a muslin cloth (cheesecloth), placed on top of a pot of boiling water and steamed for a couple of minutes. The rice paper sheet is then removed and placed on bamboo racks to dry in the sun. Watching someone make this is mesmerising; they move from batter to steamer to bamboo rack with a speed that makes it look easy, but don't be fooled!

True Vietnamese rice paper sheets are much thinner than what we buy in the supermarket, which are generally thicker and need to be rehydrated in either cold or warm water, depending on their thickness. The rice paper found in Vietnamese markets is usually rehydrated with just a light sponge of water, or moistened with fruits, such as pineapple or star fruit, when placed in the centre of the table as part of a salad.

At Annam, we import beautiful thin rice paper from the markets of Vietnam. We serve it with our whole grilled fish and steaks, as well as accompanying large herb salad plates with pineapple and granny smith apple. We encourage customers to use the fruit to moisten the rice paper before rolling, just like we do in Vietnam.

# GỎI CUỐN TÔM HÈO

Pork and prawn rice paper rolls

This is my go-to rice paper roll recipe. It's simple, it's the original and it's the best!

---

500 g (1 lb 2 oz) pork belly
1 lemongrass stalk, white part only, thinly sliced
6 garlic cloves, halved
1 long red chilli, split
50 g (1¾ oz) bun (rice noodles)
12 large round rice paper sheets
1 bunch mint, leaves picked
1 bunch Vietnamese mint, leaves picked
1 coral (frisée) lettuce, washed and trimmed
12 medium cooked prawns (shrimp), peeled
   and deveined, sliced in half lengthways

### Hoi sin dipping sauce
200 ml (7 fl oz) hoi sin sauce
50 ml (1¾ fl oz) coconut cream
1 tablespoon sriracha chilli sauce
3 tablespoons Roasted peanuts (see page 213)

**1**  Place the pork belly in a saucepan and cover with cold water. Add the lemongrass, garlic and chilli and place over high heat. Bring to the boil, then reduce the heat and simmer for 30 minutes or until the pork is cooked through. Remove the pork from the pan, set aside to cool, then slice into thin pieces.

**2**  Cook the noodles according to the packet instructions, then drain and run under cold water until cool. Set aside.

**3**  Fill a large bowl with cold water. Lay the rice paper sheets, sliced pork, cooked noodles, herbs, lettuce and prawns in front of you.

**4**  Dip one rice paper sheet in the bowl of water, turning over and making sure that the sheet is completely wet before shaking off any excess water. Lay the rice paper sheet flat on a clean workbench. Starting with the noodles, place a small quantity of each of the filling ingredients along the middle of the rice paper (I like to leave some of the lettuce poking out the ends).

**5**  Starting with the side nearest to you, carefully lift the rice paper over the filling, then roll away from you to create a tight rice paper roll. Repeat with the remaining ingredients until you have 12 rolls. Cut the rice paper rolls in half, if desired.

**6**  Place the hoi sin sauce, coconut cream and sriracha in a small saucepan over low heat and warm, stirring the ingredients to combine. Remove from the heat and divide the sauce among dipping bowls. Sprinkle the peanuts over the top and serve with the rice paper rolls.

# GỎI CUỐN TÔM CHIÊN CỐM DẸP XANH

Makes 12

Fried green rice prawn rice paper rolls

I first discovered green rice in Hanoi many years ago. It's usually eaten as a sweet steamed rice and sold by street vendors at the beginning of the rice harvest, but I like to use it as a breadcrumb-like coating for fried prawns. They add a fantastic crunchy texture to these delicate rice paper rolls but are equally delicious served on their own with nuoc mam and a herb plate.

---

170 g (6 oz/1 cup) rice flour
200 g (7 oz) green rice flakes
2 litres (2 qts) vegetable oil, for deep-frying
12 large green prawns (shrimp), peeled and deveined, tails left intact
50 g (1¾ oz) bun (rice) noodles
12 medium round rice paper sheets
½ avocado, cut into 12 slices
1 bunch mint or Vietnamese mint, leaves picked
1 coral (frisee) lettuce, washed and trimmed
Nuoc mam dipping sauce (see page 206), to serve

1  Whisk the rice flour and 125 ml (4½ fl oz/½ cup) water in a large bowl until smooth. Place the green rice flakes in a shallow bowl.

2  Heat the oil in a large saucepan to 180°C (350°F) on a kitchen thermometer.

3  Skewer each prawn onto a bamboo skewer and gentle pull the prawn to lengthen it as much as possible. Dip a prawn into the batter, then roll in the green rice flakes until completely coated. Repeat with another two prawns, then lower the bamboo sticks into the oil and cook the prawns for 2–3 minutes until golden. Remove the prawns from the oil and drain on a plate lined with paper towel. Repeat with the remaining prawns.

4  Cook the noodles according to the packet instructions, then drain and run under cold water until cool. Set aside.

5  Fill a large bowl with cold water. Lay the rice paper sheets, cooked noodles, avocado, mint, lettuce and fried prawns in front of you.

6  Dip one rice paper sheet in the bowl of water, turning over and making sure that the sheet is completely wet before shaking off any excess water. Lay the rice paper sheet flat on a clean workbench. Starting with the noodles, place a small quantity of each of the filling ingredients except the prawns along the middle of the rice paper.

7  Starting with the side nearest to you, carefully lift the rice paper over the filling, then roll the rice paper and filling away from you. Just before you finish rolling, add a prawn along the length of the roll so the tail hangs out one end, then roll up completely. Repeat with the remaining ingredients until you have 12 rice paper rolls.

8  Serve with the nuoc mam on the side for dipping.

**46**  **RICE PAPER**

# GỎI CUỐN CÁ HỐI

Salmon and apple rice paper rolls

This is my own little take on a Japanese-influenced rice paper roll using raw salmon and the crisp, sour taste of green apple. Don't be afraid to get creative when choosing ingredients for your rice paper rolls. There are almost no rules, although avoid soft fruits, as they really don't work and you'll be sorely disappointed!

12 medium round rice paper sheets
200 g (7 oz) sashimi-grade skinless salmon fillet, cut into 2 cm (¾ in) thick slices
1 mizuna lettuce, washed and trimmed
2 granny smith apples, cored and cut into matchsticks

**Wasabi mayonnaise**
125 g (4 oz/½ cup) kewpie mayonnaise
2 tablespoons wasabi paste

**1** To make the dipping sauce, combine the mayonnaise and wasabi in a bowl. Set aside.

**2** Fill a large bowl with cold water. Lay the rice paper sheets, salmon, lettuce and apple in front of you.

**3** Dip one rice paper sheet in the bowl of water, turning over and making sure that the sheet is completely wet before shaking off any excess water. Lay the rice paper sheet flat on a clean workbench. Place a few lettuce leaves and apple matchsticks along the middle of the rice paper.

**4** Starting with the edge nearest to you, carefully lift the rice paper over the filling, then roll the rice paper and filling away from you. Just before you finish rolling, add a slice of salmon along the length of the roll, then roll up completely. Repeat with the remaining ingredients until you have 12 rice paper rolls, then cut each roll into 2–3 pieces to look like rolled sushi.

**5** Top the rolls with a small dollop of wasabi mayonnaise or serve alongside the rolls in dipping bowls.

# NEM RÁN

Hanoi spring rolls

In Vietnam, spring rolls are traditionally made using rice paper instead of the thin pastry that's often used in other Southeast Asian countries and China. Fried rice paper gives a unique crunch and texture that most Vietnamese people love.

20 small rice papers sheets
2 litres (2 qts) vegetable oil, for deep-frying
Nuoc mam dipping sauce (see page 206), to serve

### Filling

50 g (1¾ oz) glass (cellophane) noodles
500 g (1 lb 2 oz) minced (ground) pork
50 g (1¾ oz) wood ear mushrooms, roughly chopped
1 tablespoon fish sauce, plus extra if needed
1 tablespoon sugar, plus extra if needed
1 teaspoon ground white pepper, plus extra if needed

### Salad plate

1 bunch mint
1 bunch Vietnamese mint
1 bunch shiso
1 iceberg lettuce, leaves separated

**1** Start by making the filling. Soak the glass noodles in a bowl of cold water for 30 minutes, then drain and snip into short pieces using kitchen scissors.

**2** In a large bowl, combine the cooked glass noodles, pork, mushroom, fish sauce, sugar and white pepper. Work the mixture together, making sure that everything is evenly mixed through. Check the seasoning by cooking 2 teaspoons of the mixture in a small frying pan over medium heat or in the microwave for 30 seconds. Taste and add more fish sauce, sugar or white pepper to the mixture, if necessary, to balance the sweet and salty flavours.

**3** Arrange the herbs and lettuce leaves on a large serving platter.

**4** Lightly spray a rice paper sheet with water, wiping off any excess liquid. Lay the rice paper sheet flat on a clean workbench. Spoon about 1 tablespoon of the filling along the centre of the rice paper, then fold in the ends and roll up tightly to make a cigar-shaped roll. Repeat with the remaining rice paper sheets and filling to make 20 spring rolls.

**5** Heat the oil in a large saucepan to 180°C (350°F) on a kitchen thermometer.

**6** Working in batches, lower a few spring rolls into the oil and cook for 10–12 minutes, until golden and crispy. Remove using a slotted spoon and drain on a plate lined with paper towel.

**7** Serve with the salad plate and nuoc mam. Place a spring roll in a lettuce leaf, top with a few herbs, then wrap it up and dip into the nuoc mam.

# CHẢ GIÒ CUA VÀ THỊT HEO

Crab and pork spring rolls

I first ate this dish a few years ago down a laneway in the Old Quarter in Hanoi. The flavours were so simple and delicious with a wonderful crispy texture. I just had to recreate it for this book!

---

20 medium rice paper sheets
2 litres (2 qts) vegetable oil, for deep-frying
Nuoc mam dipping sauce (see page 206), to serve

**Crab and pork filling**
500 g (1 lb 2 oz) minced (ground) pork
2 shallots, finely chopped
2 garlic cloves, minced
2 tablespoons fish sauce, plus extra if needed
1 tablespoon sugar, plus extra if needed
pinch of ground white pepper
50 g (1¾ oz) wood ear mushrooms, roughly chopped
300 g (10½ oz) fresh crab meat

**Salad plate**
1 iceberg lettuce or butter (bibb) lettuce,
   leaves separated
1 bunch mint, leaves picked
1 bunch Vietnamese mint, leaves picked
1 bunch shiso, leaves picked

**1**  To make the crab and pork filling, place all the ingredients except the crab meat in a large bowl and mix to combine. Check the seasoning by cooking off 2 teaspoons of the mixture in a small frying pan over medium heat or in the microwave for 30 seconds. Taste, and add more fish sauce or sugar to the mixture, if necessary, to balance the sweet and salty flavours.

**2**  Arrange the lettuce leaves and herbs on a large serving platter.

**3**  Let's make spring rolls! Lightly spray a rice paper sheet with a little water, wiping off any excess liquid. Lay the rice paper sheet flat on a clean workbench. Spoon about 1 tablespoon of the filling in the centre of the rice paper and top with two teaspoons of the crab meat. Fold in all four sides of the rice paper to make a tight square. Repeat with the remaining rice paper sheets and filling to make 20 spring rolls.

**4**  Heat the oil in a large saucepan to 180°C (350°F) on a kitchen thermometer.

**5**  Working in batches, lower a few spring rolls into the oil and cook for 7–10 minutes, until golden and crispy. Remove using a slotted spoon and drain on a plate lined with paper towel.

**6**  Serve the spring rolls with the salad plate and nuoc mam. Place a spring roll in a lettuce leaf, top with a few herbs, then wrap it all up and dip in the nuoc mam.

# BÁNH TRÁNG NƯỚNG

## Grilled rice paper

In this dish, rice paper sheets are normally grilled over a low charcoal heat, but they can also be cooked on a wire rack over a gas burner – just make sure you work quickly as the rice paper will burn if left for too long.

6 quail eggs
2 spring onions (scallions), thinly sliced
50 g (1¾ oz) toasted dried baby shrimp (see note)
4 large rice paper sheets
sriracha chilli sauce, for drizzling
kewpie mayonnaise, for drizzling

**1**　Whisk the quail eggs, spring onion and dried baby shrimp in a bowl.

**2**　Place a wire rack over a gas burner on low heat. Carefully place one rice paper sheet on the wire rack and spoon over one-quarter of the mixture. Using tongs, very carefully move the rice paper over the flame while spreading the mixture to cover the rice paper – the rice paper will change from a clear colour to white and will lightly puff up when cooked.

**3**　Once the egg is set, remove from the heat and drizzle with sriracha and kewpie. Repeat with the remaining ingredients until you have four grilled, crunchy and saucy rice papers. Consume immediately!

**Note:** Vietnamese dried baby shrimp (tom kho) are lightly toasted. You can find them in Asian supermarkets.

# BÁNH TRÁNG TRỘN

Rice paper salad with shrimp

Adding rice paper to salads is a fairly new innovation that's taken off over the last five years. The addition of rice paper to this tangy salad adds a wonderful textural element to the dish. It's also great served with Vietnamese beer!

---

120 g (4 oz) round thin rice paper sheets (see note), cut into 5 cm (2 in) wide strips
1 green mango, shredded
50 g (1¾ oz) dried baby shrimp
1 bunch Vietnamese mint, leaves picked
4 quail eggs, hard-boiled and peeled
2 tablespoons Fried shallots (see page 212)
2 tablespoons Roasted peanuts (see page 213)

**Soy and shallot dressing**
1 tablespoon vegetable oil
2 shallots, thinly sliced
120 ml (4 fl oz) soy sauce
pinch of five-spice powder
1 teaspoon fish sauce
2 tablespoons sugar

**1**   To make the soy and shallot dressing, heat the vegetable oil in a frying pan over medium heat. Add the shallot and cook for 4–5 minutes, until soft and slightly browned. Add the remaining ingredients and simmer for 2 minutes, until the sugar has dissolved. Remove from the heat and set aside.

**2**   Place the rice paper strips, mango, dried baby shrimp, mint, eggs and fried shallots in a salad bowl and toss to combine. Drizzle some of the sauce over the salad and toss again. Keep adding the dressing and tossing the salad until the dressing is all used and the rice paper has softened. Top with the peanuts and serve immediately.

**Note:** Rice paper sheets come in different thicknesses. Ask at your local Asian supermarket for the thinnest variety.

A legacy of French colonialism, the Vietnamese took the humble baguette and made it better. Crispy on the outside; light and fluffy on the inside, the banh mi is a versatile and portable meal for people on the go. It's a staple for breakfast or eaten as a quick snack throughout the day. The fillings are endless, but generally banh mi always include a rich pate and bo (mayonnaise thickened to the consistency of butter), with pickles, cucumber and spring onions (scallions) as the base ingredients. The pate is more rustic than its French counterpart, with a far greater texture achieved through the addition of bread and pork fat to help keep it rich and moist. The bo helps bind everything together, and I suggest slathering it on your banh mi to ensure an authentic flavour.

Each region of Vietnam has its own interpretation of banh mi and how it's made. In Hanoi, banh mi are long and thin with simple fillings that focus on one protein and a little coriander (cilantro) and spring onion. In Central Vietnam – especially in Hoi An – banh mi are slightly wider in the middle, but the ends come to a point. These rolls are much crispier on the outside and are filled with beautiful grilled and roasted meats, along with a drizzle of sauce from the meat and topped with a mixture of coriander and Vietnamese mint. In the south of Vietnam, and in particular Saigon, the rolls are fatter and much lighter, while maintaining a crispy exterior with an inside that's as light and soft as a cloud. These banh mi are more extravagant with lashings of bo and loads of meat, vegetables and herbs. This is the style that is most often served outside of Vietnam and the one I serve at my Pho Nom restaurants.

If you're in Vietnam and not sure which banh mi stall to try, there is one tip that I always recommend: when in doubt, follow the crowd! The best street-food stalls are the busiest for a reason, after all.

# BÁNH MÌ HEO QUAY

Roast pork belly banh mi

Roast pork belly. In a banh mi! Can there be a greater filling for a sandwich?

─────────────

4 banh mi (Vietnamese bread rolls)
Chicken liver pate (see page 208), for spreading
Vietnamese butter (see page 207), for spreading
1 tablespoon hoi sin sauce
1 Lebanese (short) cucumber, sliced into
   8 long wedges
2 spring onions (scallions), cut into 15 cm (6 in) lengths
200 g (7 oz) Pickled carrot and daikon (see page 209)
sliced bird's eye chilli, to taste
coriander (cilantro) leaves, to taste

**Pork belly**
500 g (1 lb 2 oz) pork belly
1 teaspoon five-spice powder
sea salt

**1**  Preheat the oven to 250°C (440°F).

**2**  First, roast the pork belly. Rub the meat side of the belly with the five-spice powder and season with salt. Score the skin side and rub with 2 tablespoons of salt, making sure to rough up the skin so it becomes crispy when cooked. Set aside for 5 minutes.

**3**  Wipe off any excess liquid from the meat and season with a little more salt. Transfer to a roasting tin, skin side up, and roast in the oven for 30 minutes or until the skin is crispy. Reduce the temperature to 180°C (350°F) and cook for further 30 minutes or until the pork is cooked through. Remove from the oven and rest the pork for a few minutes before slicing into thin pieces.

**4**  Slice open the banh mi along the side without cutting all the way through. Spread the bottom half generously with pate and butter, and place the sliced pork on top. Drizzle over a little hoi sin sauce and add the cucumber, spring onion and pickles. Garnish with the chilli and coriander, to taste.

# BÁNH MÌ ỐP LA

Fried egg banh mi

I remember my father used to make this for us on the weekends. He would fry all the eggs in one large frying pan, making sure the edges were crispy and drizzle them with Maggi seasoning. My brothers would be so excited, standing around with their banh mi in hand, ready to pounce on the eggs as soon as they were cooked. I could never sit down and wait, as I needed the speed to get past my brothers to get the best crunchy bits! Now I cook this for my staff at the restaurant. Thankfully, it's a bit more relaxed!

1 tablespoon vegetable oil
8 eggs
4 banh mi (Vietnamese bread rolls)
Chicken liver pate (see page 208), for spreading
  (omit for a vegetarian banh mi)
Vietnamese butter (see page 207), for spreading
200 g (7 oz) Pickled carrot and daikon (see page 209)
1 bunch coriander (cilantro)
2 spring onions (scallions), cut into 15 cm (6 in) lengths
1 Lebanese (short) cucumber, sliced into
  8 long wedges
2–4 tablespoons Maggi seasoning
sea salt and ground white pepper, to taste
sliced bird's eye chilli, to taste (optional)

**1**  Heat 1 teaspoon of the oil in a frying pan over medium–high heat. Crack in two eggs and fry, sunny side up, allowing the edges to crisp up. Drain the eggs on paper towel and repeat with the remaining oil and eggs.

**2**  Slice open the banh mi along the side without cutting all the way through. Spread the bottom half generously with pate and butter, and add the pickles, a handful of coriander, the spring onion and cucumber. Top with two fried eggs, dress with a little Maggi seasoning and season with salt and pepper. Garnish with chilli, to taste, if desired.

# BÁNH MÌ XÍU MẠI

Braised meatball banh mi

Xiu mai is a great example of a Vietnamese play on Chinese and French food influences. Meat dumplings (meatballs) are braised in a tomato sauce, then piled into a crispy banh mi with all the trimmings. This sandwich is one of my favourites to eat during the colder months.

———

4 banh mi (Vietnamese bread rolls)
Chicken liver pate (see page 208), for spreading
Vietnamese butter (see page 207), for spreading
200 g (7 oz) Pickled carrot and daikon (see page 209)
large handful of coriander (cilantro)
2 spring onions (scallions), cut into 15 cm (6 in) lengths
1 Lebanese (short) cucumber, sliced into
   8 long wedges

**Meatballs**
500 g (1 lb 2 oz) minced (ground) pork
200 g (7 oz) water chestnuts, drained and
   rinsed, finely chopped
3 spring onions (scallions), thinly sliced
3 shallots, finely chopped
2 garlic cloves, finely chopped
1 teaspoon ground white pepper
3 tablespoons fish sauce
1 tablespoon caster (superfine) sugar
1 egg

**Sauce**
3 tablespoons vegetable oil
2 garlic cloves, finely chopped
4 shallots, finely chopped
1 tomato, finely chopped
200 ml (7 fl oz) chicken stock
2 tablespoons tomato paste (concentrated puree)
2 tablespoons fish sauce
1 tablespoon caster (superfine) sugar
pinch of sea salt

**1**  To make the meatballs, place all the ingredients in a large bowl and mix well. Slap the mixture firmly against the side of the bowl to help bind the proteins together.

**2**  Line a bamboo steamer with baking paper and set over a saucepan of simmering water. Roll the pork mixture into golf ball–sized balls, then transfer to the steamer and steam for 10 minutes. Remove from the heat and set aside.

**3**  Meanwhile, to make the sauce, heat the oil in a heavy-based frying pan over medium–high heat. Add the garlic and shallot and cook for 2–3 minutes until soft, then add the tomato and cook for a further 4–5 minutes until the tomato softens and begins to collapse. Add the chicken stock, tomato paste, fish sauce, sugar and salt and bring to the boil. Add the meatballs, then reduce the heat to a simmer and cook for a further 15 minutes or until the meatballs are soft and tender and the sauce has thickened.

**4**  Slice open the banh mi along the side without cutting all the way through. Spread the bottom half generously with pate and butter, then add the pickles, coriander, spring onion and cucumber. Evenly divide the meatballs and sauce among the banh mi and serve.

# BÒ NÉ SAIGON

Saigon breakfast hotplate

I love this dish, and I eat it every time I'm in Saigon. The excitement of a sizzling hotplate arriving at the table, tearing my banh mi into pieces and topping them with small amounts of meat and salad, and then dunking them all in the egg yolk cannot be beaten! My wife likes to tear the banh mi in half to make two mini banh mi with the meat and salad stuffed inside. At our Pho Nom stores, we put all the filling inside the roll to make it easier to eat. There's no right or wrong way to eat it!

If you don't have a hotplate, you can use a frying pan instead and dish up before bringing the food to the table.

4 × 100 g (3½ oz) minute or flank steaks
sea salt and freshly cracked white pepper
100 ml (3½ fl oz) vegetable oil
4 eggs
2 onions, sliced
4 thick slices Chicken liver pate (see page 208)
4 banh mi (Vietnamese bread rolls)
Maggi seasoning, to serve

**Salad plate**
1 Lebanese (short) cucumber, sliced on an angle
1 small iceberg lettuce, leaves separated
1 tomato, sliced

**1** Season the steak with salt and pepper.

**2** Heat a large hotplate or a frying pan over medium–high heat. Pour in the oil and add the steak. Crack the eggs next to the steak and cook sunny side up. Scatter the onion on the other side of the hotplate and cook, turning, until soft. Flip the steak over and continue cooking until cooked to your liking – I recommend medium–rare.

**3** Place the pate on top of the cooked onion and season with salt and pepper. Take the hotplate to the table or divide the steak, eggs and pate-topped onion among four plates. Serve with the banh mi, salad plate and Maggi seasoning in the centre of the table, and invite everyone to help themselves.

Vietnamese people love to grill meats, fish and shellfish, and on the streets of Vietnam, you'll find ceramic grills fuelled by charcoal filling the air with clouds of smoke. The luring smells always take me back to fond food memories of delicious past experiences.

Most of the recipes in this chapter are designed to be cooked on a charcoal grill. If you don't have a grill, a barbecue or oven will give similar results, but the flavour won't be quite the same.

Cooking over charcoal adds a unique smokiness to dishes and a more intense flavour, which is a result of the rendered fat dripping from the meat onto the charcoal which, in turn, releases more flavour back onto the meat.

To light my charcoal grill, I use a chimney starter (a round hollow cylinder with a mesh grate at the bottom) to heat the charcoal. Load some paper in the cylinder followed by enough charcoal for grilling. Light the paper from the bottom and wait for the coals to heat up. When the charcoal is roaring red, it's ready to be tipped onto the grill.

There are many varieties of grill available: Webers, Japanese Konro grills and the traditional clay stoves used in Vietnam, and all will do the trick nicely. Whatever you choose, make sure it insulates the heat so your food is cooked evenly. I use a Japanese Konro because the heat is well regulated and it doesn't get too hot to touch from the outside. When I'm finished with the charcoal, I usually place it in a pot and cover with a lid to slowly put the charcoal out. I then put this aside to use again.

# BÒ LÁ LỐT

Grilled beef wrapped in betel leaf

Bo la lot are perfectly wrapped beef parcels in betel leaves. When cooked over a charcoal grill, the smell of grilled betel leaf is incredibly fragrant. These really are a must-have at any barbecue.

---

1 kg (2 lb 3 oz) minced (ground) beef
100 g (3½ oz) minced (ground) pork fat
100 ml (3½ fl oz) oyster sauce
4 garlic cloves, minced
2 lemongrass stalks, white part only, minced
1 teaspoon dried chilli flakes
2 tablespoons caster (superfine) sugar
2 tablespoons fish sauce
48 betel leaves

**To serve**
1 iceberg lettuce, leaves separated
1 bunch Vietnamese mint
1 bunch mint
Nuoc mam dipping sauce (see page 206)

**1**  Soak 12 bamboo skewers in cold water for 1 hour. Drain.

**2**  Combine the beef and pork fat in a large bowl and mix well. Add the remaining ingredients except the betel leaves and form the mixture into a ball. Slap the ball against the side of the bowl several times until the mixture no longer sticks to your fingers. Cover with plastic wrap and set aside to rest for 30–60 minutes.

**3**  Prepare a charcoal grill or preheat a barbecue grill to high.

**4**  Place a betel leaf on a chopping board and roll 30 g–40 g (1 oz–1½ oz) of the beef mixture in your hands. Place the mixture in the centre of the leaf and gently roll into a sausage shape just smaller than the width of the leaf. Fold in the ends of the leaf and roll into a tight log, then push a bamboo skewer through the centre to secure the leaf and its filling. Repeat with the remaining filling and betel leaves, pushing four bo la lot onto each skewer.

**5**  When the charcoal grill is ready (the embers should be glowing red with a small flame on the charcoal), place the bo la lot on the grill and cook, turning from time to time, for about 8 minutes or until the rolls are firm when squeezed with tongs.

**6**  Place the lettuce and herbs in the centre of the table and divide the nuoc mam among dipping bowls. Invite guests to wrap the bo la lot and herbs in the lettuce leaves, and dip them in the nuoc mam.

# BÚN CHẢ HANOI

Chargrilled pork patties with herbs and noodles

The first time I was served this dish in Hanoi, I wasn't quite sure how to eat it, and it turned out to be the complete opposite of how you would eat bun (rice noodles) in the south. The herbs and bun were served seperately alongside a bowl of grilled meats in a nuoc mam broth. Should I eat them together like we do in the south? No, you are supposed to use your chopsticks to grab some noodles and herbs, then dip them in the nuoc mam broth and slurp it down before digging back in for some meat. The results were super delicious.

---

500 g (1 lb 2 oz) minced (ground) pork
50 g (1¾ oz) minced (ground) pork fat
500 g (1 lb 2 oz) pork belly, thinly sliced
100 g (3½ oz) thin bun (rice noodles)
250 ml (8½ fl oz/1 cup) Chicken broth (see page 146 or use store-bought)
250 ml (8½ fl oz/1 cup) Nuoc mam dipping sauce (see page 206)

**Marinade**
200 ml (7 fl oz) fish sauce
100 g (3½ oz) caster (superfine) sugar
1–3 garlic cloves, minced
5 shallots, minced
3 tablespoons vegetable oil
pinch of ground white pepper

**Pickles**
200 g (7 oz) green papaya, thinly sliced
1 carrot, thinly sliced
200 ml (7 fl oz) pickle liquid (see page 209)

**Salad**
1 bunch mint
1 bunch Vietnamese mint
1 bunch shiso (optional)

**1** Combine the marinade ingredients in a small bowl.

**2** Place the minced pork and pork fat in a large bowl and the pork belly in another bowl. Pour half the marinade over the pork mince and pork fat, and mix well to combine. Slap the mixture against the side of the bowl a few times to remove any air (this helps to prevent the mixture from falling apart when grilled). Set aside in the fridge to marinate for at least 3 hours or, preferably, overnight.

**3** Pour the other half of the marinade over the pork belly. Mix well and set aside in the fridge.

**4** To prepare the pickles, place the green papaya and carrot in a bowl. Pour over the pickle liquid, ensuring the ingredients are fully submerged, and set aside for 2 hours.

**5** Roll the minced pork mixture into golf ball–sized balls, then return to the fridge for 1–2 hours to firm up.

**6** Prepare a charcoal grill. You can use a barbecue grill for this dish, but you won't achieve that smoky flavour.

**7** Cook the noodles according to the packet instructions. Drain and rinse under cold running water, then drain again and set aside.

**8** Warm the chicken broth in a saucepan over medium heat.

**9** When the charcoal grill is ready (the embers should be glowing red with a small flame on the charcoal), slightly flatten the meatballs using the palms of your hands, then transfer to the grill. Carefully add the pork belly, being careful of flare-ups from the fat dripping onto the charcoal, which will make the meat black and bitter-tasting. Cook the meatballs and pork belly, turning regularly, for 7–10 minutes until cooked through.

**10** To serve, place the cooked noodles and salad ingredients on a large serving plate. Drain the pickles and evenly divide among small bowls. Add the meatballs and pork belly and evenly pour over the warmed chicken broth and nuoc mam.

**11** Invite guests to dip a few noodles and herbs into their broth and eat, followed by mouthfuls of the meat and pickles. Enjoy!

# CÁ NƯỚNG CUỐN BÁNH TRÁNG
Grilled fish in rice paper

Grilled fish is very common in Vietnam, and it's often served wrapped in fresh herbs with cucumber and pineapple to give different flavours and textures.

I've used cod in this recipe, but you can substitute any other firm white fish, or even just use fish fillets if you don't want to deal with the head and the bones.

---

1 × 400 g–600 g (14 oz–1 lb 5 oz) whole firm white fish, such as Murray cod, seabass, snapper or flounder, gutted and cleaned
100 g (3½ oz) vermicelli bun (rice noodles)
sea salt
vegetable oil, for rubbing
2 tablespoons Fried shallots (see page 212)
30 g (1 oz) Roasted peanuts (see page 213)
50 ml (1¾ fl oz) Spring onion oil (see page 207)
80 ml (2½ fl oz) Nuoc mam dipping sauce (see page 206)
50 g (1¾ oz) Pickled carrot and daikon (see page 209)
12 medium round rice paper sheets

## Salad plate
1 bunch Vietnamese mint
1 bunch mint
1 bunch shiso
½ pineapple, peeled, cored and thinly sliced
2 Lebanese (short) cucumbers, cut into batons

**1** Using a sharp knife, butterfly the fish by laying it flat on a chopping board and carefully slicing from the tail to the bottom fin along the inside of the belly up to the spine. Flip the fish over and repeat the process. Open up the fish and, using a pair of kitchen scissors, cut away the spine from the tail to the neck of the fish, leaving the head and tail intact. Remove any remaining bones, then use a cleaver to slice most of the way through the head. flatten out the fish and trim the wings and fins.

**2** Prepare a charcoal grill or preheat a barbecue grill to high. Alternatively, preheat the oven to 180°C (350°F).

**3** Cook the noodles according to the packet instructions, then drain and run under cold water until cool. Drain again and set aside.

**4** Arrange the salad ingredients on a large serving platter.

**5** When the charcoal grill is ready (the embers should be glowing red with a small flame on the charcoal), season both sides of the fish with sea salt and rub with vegetable oil. Place the fish on the grill, skin side down, and cook for 5–7 minutes until the skin is crispy, then flip and cook for a further 5–7 minutes until the fish is cooked through.

**6** Transfer the fish to a plate, skin side up, sprinkle over the fried shallots and roasted peanuts, and drizzle with the spring onion oil. Combine the nuoc mam and pickles in a bowl, then divide between two dipping bowls (see note).

**7** Arrange a large bowl of water, the noodles, dipping bowls, rice paper sheets, salad plate and fish in the centre of the table. To eat, grab a rice paper sheet and moisten with a little water. Lay the rice paper on a plate and fill with a few herbs, slices of pineapple, cucumber and a little of the fish. Roll into a tight roll and dip into the nuoc mam and pickles. Enjoy!

**Note:** Traditionally, this dish is served with mam nem, a fermented anchovy dipping sauce, which is not for the faint-hearted! If you'd like to give it a go, check out the recipe on page 215.

# BÚN THỊT NƯỚNG
Grilled pork and vermicelli noodle salad

Vermicelli noodle salads make a fantastic quick meal and are perfect in the hotter months. This dish is the South Vietnamese version of bun cha (see page 80).

600 g (1 lb 5 oz) boneless pork shoulder, thinly sliced
200 g (7 oz) vermicelli bun (rice noodles)
½ butter (bibb) lettuce, shredded (optional)
2 Lebanese (short) cucumbers, julienned
150 g (5½ oz) Pickled carrot and daikon
 (see page 209)
2 tablespoons Fried shallots (see page 212)
80 ml (2½ fl oz/⅓ cup) Spring onion oil (see page 207)
1 bunch mint, leaves picked
1 bunch Vietnamese mint, leaves picked
100 g (3½ oz) Roasted peanuts (see page 213)
Nuoc mam dipping sauce (see page 206), to serve

**Marinade**
2 shallots, finely chopped
2 garlic cloves, finely chopped
1 tablespoon honey
3 tablespoons fish sauce
3 tablespoons vegetable oil
1 tablespoon caster (superfine) sugar

**1**  Combine the marinade ingredients in a large bowl and stir until the sugar and honey have dissolved. Add the pork and mix well. Set aside in the fridge to marinade for at least 4 hours or, preferably, overnight.

**2**  Prepare a charcoal grill or preheat a barbecue grill to medium–high.

**3**  Cook the noodles according to the packet instructions, then drain and run under cold water until cool. Drain again and set aside.

**4**  When the charcoal grill is ready (the embers should be glowing red with a small flame on the charcoal), place the pork on the grill and cook, turning frequently, for 8–10 minutes until golden brown. Transfer to a plate.

**5**  Divide the noodles among four bowls and add the lettuce (if using), cucumber and pickles. Top with the pork and fried shallots and drizzle over the spring onion oil. Garnish with a handful of herbs and serve with the peanuts and nuoc mam on the side, to add as you wish.

# MỰC NƯỚNG MUỐI ỘT

Chilli salt calamari

I love to fish for calamari when I get the chance, and this dish is the best way to eat it when it's fresh from the ocean. It's super easy to cook on a charcoal grill, which also helps to retain the flavour and sweetness of the calamari. Give it a go!

2 × 500 g (1 lb 2 oz) whole calamari, cleaned and rinsed, hoods and tentacles separated (ask your fishmonger to do this for you)
cooking oil spray
Green chilli dipping sauce (see page 214), to serve

**Chilli salt**
50 g (1¾ oz) long red chillies
2 garlic cloves
30 g (1 oz) sea salt

**Salad plate**
½ bunch mint
½ bunch Vietnamese mint
1 butter (bibb) lettuce, leaves separated (optional)

**1** Preheat the oven to 100°C (210°F). Line a baking tray with baking paper.

**2** To make the chilli salt, use a mortar and pestle to pound the chillies and garlic to a paste. Add the salt and pound until well combined. Transfer the mixture to the prepared tray, spread out in an even layer and dry in the oven for 20 minutes. Keep an eye on the salt, moving the mixture around every 5–7 minutes so that the salt dries evenly and doesn't burn. Remove from the oven and set aside to cool.

**3** Prepare a charcoal grill or preheat a barbecue grill to high. Spray the calamari with a little cooking oil and sprinkle with the chilli salt.

**4** When the charcoal grill is ready (the embers should be glowing red with a small flame on the charcoal), place the calamari on the grill and cook each side for 3–5 minutes until the flesh turns white. Be careful not to overcook the calamari; otherwise it will be tough.

**5** Transfer the calamari to a serving plate, and place in the centre of the table, along with a serving platter of the herbs and lettuce (if using) and green chilli dipping sauce. Slice the calamari hoods into rings and the tentacles into smaller pieces. Invite guests to wrap pieces of calamari in the herbs and lettuce and dip into the green chilli dipping sauce.

# BẦP NƯỚNG PHÔ MAI

Grilled sweet corn with Laughing Cow cheese

Grilled sweet corn is sold throughout Vietnam as a street-food snack. This is my take on the classic, adding kewpie mayo and Laughing Cow cheese into the mix. It makes a great side dish at any barbecue.

---

2 lap cheong sausages, finely diced
4 sweet corn cobs, husks and silks removed
80 g (2¾ oz) kewpie mayonnaise
4 triangles Laughing Cow cheese
3 tablespoons Spring onion oil (see page 207)

**1** Prepare a charcoal grill or preheat a barbecue grill to high.

**2** Heat a small frying pan over medium heat and add the lap cheong. Cook for 5–7 minutes until the fat has rendered and the sausage is crisp. Drain on a plate lined with paper towel.

**3** When the charcoal grill is ready (the embers should be glowing red with a small flame on the charcoal), place the corn on the grill and cook, turning regularly, for 12–15 minutes until lightly charred and blistered.

**4** Combine the kewpie mayonnaise and cheese in a bowl and mix until smooth. Transfer to a plate and roll the grilled corn in the cheese mixture to give it a nice, thin coating, then roll in the lap cheong.

**5** Transfer the corn to a serving plate and drizzle with the spring onion oil. Serve immediately.

# ĐIỆP NƯỚNG MỠ HÀNH

Grilled scallops

I love eating grilled shellfish and sea snails when I'm in Vietnam. This is a simple recipe with gentle flavours that don't overpower the delicate taste of the scallops.

---

60 ml (2 fl oz/¼ cup) Spring onion oil (see page 207)
2 tablespoons fish sauce
1 teaspoon caster (superfine) sugar
12 scallops in their shells
2 tablespoons Fried shallots (see page 212)
2 tablespoons Roasted peanuts (see page 213)

**1**   Prepare a charcoal barbecue or preheat a barbecue grill to high.

**2**   Combine the spring onion oil, fish sauce and sugar in a bowl. Stir until the sugar dissolves.

**3**   Divide the spring onion oil mixture evenly among the scallop shells.

**4**   When the charcoal grill is ready (the embers should be glowing red with a small flame on the charcoal), place the scallops on the grill and cook for 5–7 minutes until cooked through.

**5**   Top with the fried shallots and peanuts and serve immediately.

BIA
BIA
BIA

Bia hoi, meaning fresh beer, is freshly brewed beer that is light and crisp – a perfect thirst quencher in the heat. It is enjoyed with friends and served alongside dishes eaten as a progressive meal.

The most famous bia hoi is in Hanoi's Old Quarter at an intersection lovingly known as Bia Hoi Corner. A visit there is recommended when in town, as the beer is always fresh and the view entertaining.

Bia hoi halls fill up with office workers at the end of the day. It's an opportunity to catch up with friends, eat, drink and laugh, and forget about the stresses of the day. If drinking at a bia hoi hall you must loudly toast by clinking glasses and chanting 'mot, hai, ba, yo!', which means one, two, three, cheers! This ruckus can often be heard from the streets outside the halls.

The dishes in this chapter are some of my favourite meals to eat with bia hoi.

# CHEM CHÉP HẤP BIA VÀ LÀ QUÊ

Serves 4

Mussels in Thai Basil and Bia Hanoi

This dish is simple and effective, with beautiful flavours coming from the Thai basil and lemongrass alongside the sweetness of the mussels. This dish is an absolute must while sitting on small plastic furniture in Vietnam!

---

1 × 330 ml (11 fl oz) can Bia Hanoi (or lager)
4 sprigs Thai basil, stalks and leaves separated
4 cm (1¾ in) piece of ginger, crushed
1 long red chilli, sliced
1 lemongrass stalk, white part only, lightly crushed and cut into 10 cm (4 in) lengths
1 kg (2 lb 3 oz) mussels, scrubbed and debearded
4 banh mi (Vietnamese rolls) (optional)

**Cumquat chilli salt**
1 bird's eye chilli
1 tablespoon sea salt
4 cumquats, halved

**1** To make the cumquat chilli salt, pound the chilli to a paste using a mortar and pestle. Add the salt and lightly pound until well combined. Divide the chilli salt among four small dipping bowls and top with two cumquat halves.

**2** Place the Bia Hanoi, Thai basil stalks, ginger, chilli and lemongrass in a saucepan large enough to comfortably hold the mussels. Cover with a lid and bring to the boil for 2–3 minutes.

**3** Add the mussels, then cover and cook, shaking the pan often, for about 5 minutes or until the shells have opened. Using a slotted spoon, transfer the mussels to a large serving plate and pour the broth into a serving bowl. Scatter the reserved Thai basil leaves over the mussels and broth.

**4** To serve, invite guests to juice the cumquats into their chilli salt. Dip the mussels in the broth followed by the chili salt, and enjoy.

98    BIA HOI

# MỰC RANG MUỐI

Five-spice calamari

This fried calamari dish is one of the greatest meals you can eat while drinking beer and catching up with mates while trading travel stories.

---

½ teaspoon five-spice powder
1 teaspoon salt
1 teaspoon caster (superfine) sugar
500 g (1 lb 2 oz) calamari hoods, cleaned and rinsed
vegetable oil, for deep-frying and frying
1 egg, beaten
½ green capsicum (bell pepper), diced
½ red capsicum (bell pepper), diced
1 small onion, diced
2 garlic cloves, minced
2 bird's eye chillies, roughly chopped, plus
   extra to garnish

### Batter
170 g (6 oz/1 cup) rice flour
100 ml (3½ fl oz) soda water (club soda)

**1**  Combine the five-spice powder, salt and sugar in a bowl and set aside.

**2**  To make the batter, place the rice flour in a bowl and slowly add the soda water, gently whisking with a fork until the batter is smooth and runny. Set aside.

**3**  Using a knife, gently score the calamari hoods in a criss-cross pattern, then cut the calamari into medium triangles.

**4**  Heat 2 litres (2 qts) of oil in a wok or large saucepan over medium–high heat until it reaches 180°C (350°F) on a kitchen thermometer.

**5**  Working in batches, dip the calamari in the beaten egg followed by the batter, allowing any excess batter to drip off. Gently lower the calamari into the hot oil and cook for 4–5 minutes until golden brown. Remove using a slotted spoon and drain on a plate lined with paper towel. Repeat with the remaining calamari.

**6**  Heat 1 tablespoon of oil in a frying pan over medium–high heat. Sauté the capsicum, onion, garlic and chilli for 2–3 minutes until the capsicum is just soft, then quickly toss through the fried calamari. Season with the reserved spice mix.

**7**  Serve immediately, garnished with extra chilli.

# CUA HẤP CHẤM NƯỚC MẮM ỚT XANH

Steamed crab with green chilli dipping sauce

Vietnamese people love eating shellfish, especially crab. It may be fiddly and a little messy, but it's all part of the experience of drinking bia hoi and slowly grazing on food. Flavoursome crab is always available at bia hoi halls. It's also one of my favourites.

---

6 × 200 g–300 g (7 oz–10½ oz) whole crabs, such as blue swimmer, spanner or mud crabs
2 lemongrass stalks, white part only, bruised
2 long red chillies, bruised
Green chilli dipping sauce (see page 214), to serve
4 cumquats, halved, to serve (optional)

**1** Set a large bamboo steamer over a saucepan of boiling water. Add the crabs, lemongrass and chilli, cover with the lid and steam for 15 minutes or until the crab is cooked through.

**2** Place the crabs on a large serving plate and invite people to dig in, dipping the meat into the green chilli dipping sauce and squeezing over the cumquat halves (if using).

# BÒ NƯỚNG VỈ

Beef cooked on a hotplate

This fantastic beef dish is cooked on a hotplate at the table and served alongside fragrant herbs, noodles and rice paper. Whenever we eat it, my uncle always says we have to duck to avoid the splatters from the hotplate! Give it a go and see for yourself.

---

2 lemongrass stalks, white part only, thinly sliced
2 bird's eye chillies, thinly sliced
3 garlic cloves, thinly sliced
80 ml (2½ fl oz/⅓ cup) fish sauce
2 tablespoons caster (superfine) sugar
50 ml (1¾ fl oz) vegetable oil
1.5 kg (3 lb 5 oz) boneless beef sirloin, thinly sliced
200 g (7 oz) bun (rice noodles)
150 ml (5 fl oz) Nuoc mam dipping sauce
   (see page 206)
100 g (3½ oz) Pickled carrot and daikon
   (see page 209)
15–20 medium round rice paper sheets
1 tablespoon butter

**Salad plate**
3 tablespoons Fried shallots (see page 212)
2 bunches mint
2 bunches Vietnamese mint
2 red apples, cored, halved and sliced
1 small pineapple, peeled, cored and sliced into rounds

1   Combine the lemongrass, chilli, garlic, fish sauce, sugar and vegetable oil in a large bowl, and stir until the sugar has dissolved. Add the beef, mix well and set aside in the fridge to marinate for 3 hours.

2   Cook the noodles according to the packet instructions, then drain and run under cold water until cool. Drain again and set aside.

3   Place all the salad plate ingredients and cooked noodles on a serving platter. Combine the nuoc mam and pickles in a bowl, then divide among dipping bowls. Pile the rice paper sheets on a plate and set a large bowl of water on the table.

4   Set up a portable gas stove and hotplate in the centre of the table and heat over medium–high heat. Melt a little of the butter on the hotplate, add a few slices of marinated beef and cook for 2–3 minutes until just cooked through. Invite guests to help themselves, and continue to cook the remaining beef in small batches as you eat.

5   To eat, invite guests to rehydrate rice paper sheets in water, then fill with the noodles, salad ingredients and beef. Roll up the rice paper and dip into the nuoc mam and pickles.

Vietnamese salads are refreshing and full of flavour, with crunchy textures, fragrant herbs and punchy dressings. Vietnamese dishes are almost always accompanied by a salad, and they are considered an integral part of any meal, providing a freshness that revitalises the palate when served with soups, grilled meats or heavier stews. Salads can range from the simplicity of a small twist of shredded cucumber or carrot, to salad plates filled with fresh herbs, lettuce, bean sprouts, fried shallots and chilli that help liven up the family meal. They are also eaten as standalone dishes, purchased freshly made from street vendors and hastily eaten while on the run, providing a cooling moment in Vietnam's intense humid heat.

Texture, texture, texture is the hallmark of Vietnamese salads, and ingredients are layered and added until the perfect balance of crunchy, chewy and soft is achieved – along with that all-important sour, sweet and salty flavour. Crunchy elements might include sour fruits, such as green papaya or mango, banana blossom or the humble cabbage and carrot. These are balanced with soft herbs, such as Thai basil, Vietnamese mint and shiso, while protein comes in many forms and might include rare beef, jellyfish or tofu. The salad is then rounded off with a nuoc mam dressing or even a creamy coconut sauce.

In this chapter, you'll find some of my favourite Vietnamese salads that can be found at street stalls up and down the country.

# BÁNH TẰM BÌ

Noodles with shredded pork and coconut cream

My wife absolutey loves this dish! She says it's the perfect balance, bringing together great-textured noodles, fresh herbs, pork (who doesn't like pork?!) and creaminess from the coconut cream. It's a great noodle salad that's worth the time and effort to make.

---

300 g (10½ oz) vermicelli bun (rice noodles)
180 g (6½ oz/2 cups) blanched bean sprouts
1 butter (bibb) lettuce, shredded
1 Lebanese (short) cucumber, julienned
60 ml (2 fl oz/¼ cup) Spring onion oil (see page 207)
handful of herbs, such as mint and Vietnamese mint, roughly chopped
200 g (7 oz) Pickled carrot and daikon (see page 209)
50 g (1¾ oz) Fried shallots (see page 212)
250 ml (8½ fl oz/1 cup) Nuoc mam dipping sauce (see page 206)

### Shredded pork (see note)

500 g (1 lb 2 oz) boneless pork shoulder
100 g (3½ oz) jasmine rice
50 g (1¾ oz) thinly sliced pig skin (see note)
2 garlic cloves, minced
1 tablespoon caster (superfine) sugar
1 tablespoon salt
3 tablespoons Garlic oil (see page 212)

### Coconut cream

500 ml (17 fl oz/2 cups) coconut milk
1 teaspoon caster (superfine) sugar
1 teaspoon salt

**1** Start by making the shredded pork. Bring a large saucepan of water to the boil, add the pork and cook for 40 minutes. Remove the pork from the pan and plunge into a bowl of iced water to cool. Drain and pat dry with paper towel.

**2** Meanwhile, gently toast the jasmine rice in a dry frying pan over medium heat, stirring often, for 20–30 minutes until golden brown. Remove from the pan and allow to cool, then grind to a powder in a food processor.

**3** Cook the noodles according to the packet instructions, then drain and run under cold water until cool. Drain again and set aside.

**4** Make the coconut cream by warming the coconut milk in a saucepan over medium heat. Add the sugar and salt and stir until dissolved. Simmer for 10 minutes or until the milk has thickened to a cream consistency.

**5** Cut the pork into matchstick-sized pieces, so it looks shredded. Rinse the pig skin under cold water and drain. In a bowl, combine the pork and pig skin with the ground toasted rice, garlic, sugar, salt and garlic oil.

**6** To serve, divide the bean sprouts among four serving bowls. Top with the noodles and shredded pork and generously drizzle over the coconut cream. Finish with the shredded lettuce, cucumber, spring onion oil, herbs, pickles and fried shallots. Serve with the nuoc mam on the side for drizzling over.

**Notes:** The shredded pork in this dish is a great accompaniment to many Vietnamese dishes – from other noodle dishes to banh mi – so feel free to experiment with it!

Prepared pig skin can be purchased from Asian butchers. It is basically pork skin with the fat removed, that's then boiled and sliced super thin.

# GỎI TÔM BƯỞI

Serves 4

Prawn and pomelo salad

The pomelo is an ancient citrus fruit native to Southeast Asia. It is not dissimilar to grapefruit, and it makes a regular appearance in Vietnamese salads. In this dish, the pomelo gives a refreshing burst of sweetness and a slight sour tang, which provides a wonderful contrast to the meaty prawns.

---

1 small pomelo
12 cooked medium prawns (shrimp), peeled and deveined
1 bunch mint, leaves picked
1 bunch Vietnamese mint, leaves picked
2 Thai basil stalks, leaves picked
150 g (5½ oz) Pickled carrot and daikon (see page 209)
2 long red chillies, deseeded and julienned
2 Lebanese (short) cucumbers, halved lengthways and sliced on an angle
2 tablespoons Fried shallots (see page 212)

**Nuoc mam dressing**
150 ml (5 fl oz) Nuoc mam dipping sauce (see page 206)
2 garlic cloves, minced
1 bird's eye chilli, thinly sliced

**1** To remove the flesh from the pomelo, peel the rind from the fruit and break the fruit in half. Individually peel the skin from each segment and gently pull the flesh out. This will ensure that the segments are not broken and bruised. Gently tear the segments into bite-sized pieces.

**2** Whisk the dressing ingredients in a small bowl.

**3** Combine all the salad ingredients except the fried shallots in a large bowl. Toss through the nuoc mam dressing, then transfer to a large serving plate or bowl.

**4** Top with the fried shallots and serve.

SALADS

# GỎI ĐU ĐỦ TÔM THỊT

Prawn and pork salad with green papaya

Green papaya is commonly used in salads throughout Southeast Asia, and this classic Vietnamese dish is no exception. It's simple, delicious and filled with multiple textures.

———————————

200 g (7 oz) pork belly
sea salt
1 litre (34 fl oz/4 cups) vegetable oil, for deep-frying
16 prawn crackers
12 cooked medium prawns (shrimp), peeled and deveined
½ small green papaya, shredded
1 bunch Thai basil, leaves picked
1 bunch shiso, thinly sliced (optional)
1 bunch Vietnamese mint, leaves picked
100 g (3½ oz) Pickled carrot and daikon (see page 209)
3 tablespoons Roasted peanuts (see page 213)

**Nuoc mam dressing**
200 ml (7 fl oz) Nuoc mam dipping sauce (see page 206)
2 garlic cloves, minced
2 bird's eye chillies, thinly sliced

**1**  Place the pork belly in a saucepan and cover with cold water. Season with salt, bring to the boil and cook for 20 minutes or until cooked through. Drain and plunge the pork into iced water to stop the cooking process. Drain on paper towel, then slice into thin pieces.

**2**  Whisk the dressing ingredients in a small bowl.

**3**  Heat the oil in a large saucepan over medium–high heat to 180°C (350°F) on a kitchen thermometer. Working in batches, fry the prawn crackers for a few seconds until puffed up and doubled in size. Using a slotted spoon, remove the crackers from the oil and drain on a plate lined with paper towel.

**4**  Combine the prawns, pork, papaya, herbs and pickles in a large bowl and toss through the dressing.

**5**  Transfer the salad to a large serving plate or bowl and top with the peanuts. Lay the prawn crackers around the salad and serve immediately.

# GỎI SỨA THỊT VỊT

Jellyfish and duck salad

Jellyfish and duck might sound like a crazy combination, but the textures work brilliantly together in this dish. As jellyfish has no distinctive flavour of its own, it absorbs the flavour of the dressing, while providing a completely unique texture to the salad that's impossible to replicate.

---

200 g (7 oz) sliced jellyfish (see note)
3 duck breasts, skin on
sea salt
2 tablespoons vegetable oil
1 bunch mint, leaves picked
1 bunch Vietnamese mint, leaves picked
1 Lebanese (short) cucumber, cut in half lengthways
   and sliced
100 g (3½ oz) Pickled carrot and daikon (see
   page 209)
100 g (3½ oz) bean sprouts
3 tablespoons Fried shallots (see page 212)

**Galangal dressing**
200 ml (7 fl oz) Nuoc mam dipping sauce (see
   page 206)
2 bird's eye chillies, thinly sliced
2 garlic cloves, minced
5 cm (2 in) piece of galangal, julienned

**1**  Rinse the jellyfish under cold running water for 10 minutes. Drain on a plate lined with paper towel.

**2**  Whisk the dressing ingredients in a small bowl.

**3**  Score the skin of the duck breasts, and season the skin with salt. Remove any sinew on the flesh side.

**4**  Heat the oil in a frying pan over medium–high heat and add the duck breasts, skin side down. Cook the duck for 7 minutes until brown, then turn over and cook for a further 5 minutes. Remove from the pan and rest for 5 minutes, then slice into thin pieces.

**5**  Combine the jellyfish, duck, herbs, cucumber, pickles and bean sprouts in a large bowl and toss through the dressing. Transfer to a large serving dish or bowl, top with the fried shallots and serve.

**Note:** Sliced jellyfish can be purchased in vacuumed packs from Asian supermarkets.

# GỎI BẮP CHUỐI TÀU HỦ CHIÊN

Banana blossom and crispy tofu salad

Banana blossom features in many Vietnamese dishes. It's often added to soups and salads, as it's excellent at absorbing flavours and providing crunch. Here, I've paired it with soft tofu for a textural hit that's hard to beat.

1 lemon
1 banana blossom
2 litres (2 qts) vegetable oil, for deep-frying
1 packet soft (but not silken) tofu, thinly sliced
4 Vietnamese sesame rice crackers
1 bunch mint, leaves picked
1 bunch shiso, leaves picked
1 long red chilli, deseeded and julienned
1 Lebanese (short) cucumber, cut into matchsticks
3 tablespoons Roasted peanuts (see page 213)
2 tablespoons Fried shallots (see page 212)

**Citrus–soy dressing**
100 ml (3½ fl oz) white or light soy sauce
100 ml (3½ fl oz) coconut water
2 bird's eye chillies, thinly sliced
30 ml (1 fl oz) freshly squeezed lime juice

**1**   Fill a large bowl with water and squeeze in the lemon.

**2**   To prepare the banana blossom, peel and discard the outer layers and flowers until you reach the light-coloured interior. Cut the blossom in half lengthways and remove the inner flowers. Thinly slice the blossom and immediately plunge into the lemon water to prevent it discolouring. Drain and run under cold running water for 5–10 minutes to wash off all the sap. Drain and set aside.

**3**   Whisk the dressing ingredients in a small bowl.

**4**   Heat the oil in a wok or large saucepan over medium–high heat to 180°C (350°F) on a kitchen thermometer. Working in batches, deep-fry the tofu for 2–3 minutes until crispy. Using a slotted spoon, remove from the oil and drain on a plate lined with paper towel.

**5**   Meanwhile, toast the rice crackers by placing a wire rack over a gas burner on low heat. Carefully place one rice cracker on the wire rack and, using tongs, very carefully move the rice paper over the flame – the rice paper will change from a clear colour to white and will lightly puff up when cooked. Repeat with the remaining rice crackers. Transfer to a large plate.

**6**   Place the banana blossom, tofu, herbs, chilli and cucumber in a large bowl. Toss the dressing through the salad, then transfer to a serving bowl. Top with the peanuts and fried shallots and serve immediately with the sesame crackers on the side.

# GỎI GÀ

Poached chicken slaw

This dish is *the* go-to Vietnamese salad that never fails to please everyone. It's quick to put together and thoroughly delicious.

———————————————————

2 lemongrass stalks, white part only, bruised
4 long red chillies
4 large chicken breasts, skin on
2 litres (2 qts) vegetable oil, for deep-frying
16 prawn crackers
200 ml (7 fl oz) Nuoc mam dipping sauce (see page 206)
30 g (1 oz) Fried shallots (see page 212)

### Slaw

200 g (7 oz) white cabbage, thinly sliced
100 g (3½ oz) red cabbage, thinly sliced
150 g (5½ oz) Pickled carrot and daikon (see page 209)
1 bunch mint, leaves picked
1 bunch Vietnamese mint, leaves picked
1 bunch shiso, leaves picked

**1**  Fill a large saucepan with 2 litres (2 qts) water and add the lemongrass and 1 chilli. Place over medium–high heat and bring to the boil. Add the chicken and poach for 30 minutes or until cooked through. To test if the chicken is cooked, insert a skewer into the thickest part of the breast; if the juices run clear, the chicken is cooked. Drain the chicken and set aside to cool. Discard the lemongrass and chilli.

**2**  Heat the oil in a large saucepan over medium–high heat to 180°C (350°F) on a kitchen thermometer. Working in batches, fry the prawn crackers for a few seconds until puffed up and doubled in size. Using a slotted spoon, remove the crackers from the oil and drain on a plate lined with paper towel.

**3**  Remove and discard the chicken skin and, using your hands, shred the meat into small pieces.

**4**  Thinly slice the remaining chillies.

**5**  Combine the slaw ingredients in a serving bowl and top with the shredded chicken. Dress the salad with the nuoc mam and arrange the prawn crackers around the edge. Top with the sliced chilli and the shallots and serve.

# GỎI BÒ TÁI CHANH

Rare beef salad

This salad is essentially a beef ceviche with a beautiful citrus flavour from the lemon. If you prefer, you could quickly blanch the beef before tossing with the lemon juice.

---

800 g (1 lb 12 oz) beef eye fillet or sirloin, thinly sliced
300 ml (10 fl oz) lemon juice
1 Lebanese (short) cucumber, halved lengthways and sliced on an angle
1 bunch Vietnamese mint, leaves picked
1 red onion, thinly sliced
150 g (5½ oz) Pickled carrot and daikon (see page 209) (optional)
3 tablespoons Fried shallots (see page 212)
3 tablespoons Roasted peanuts (see page 213)

**Ceviche dressing**
100 ml (3½ fl oz) Nuoc mam dipping sauce (see page 206)
3 bird's eye chillies, thinly sliced
2 garlic cloves, crushed
30 ml (1 fl oz) freshly squeezed lime juice, strained

**1** Place the beef in a non-reactive bowl and pour over the lemon juice. Mix well to completely coat the beef. Set aside for 7–10 minutes to allow the juice to partially cook the beef.

**2** Whisk the dressing ingredients in a small bowl.

**3** Transfer the beef to a serving bowl, shaking off any excess lemon juice. Add the cucumber, mint, onion and pickles (if using) and mix well to combine. Toss through the dressing, then transfer to a serving dish, top with the fried shallots and peanuts and serve.

Who would think that noodle soup could be such a popular part of the food scene in a country as hot as Vietnam? Each region, town and even village have their own variations. All of these come together on the streets of major cities, as people move there for a better living. Many of these are the dishes I crave when I return home from Vietnam; dishes ranging from light broths with spicy aromas to strong-flavoured fermented fish soups.

The most famous Vietnamese noodle soup is, of course, pho. It is the heart and soul of a Vietnamese breakfast and feels like a hug from deep down inside on a cold day. For me, pho brings warmth and joy, not only from the dish itself but also from gathering with family to share large bowls of this special meal.

Pho is a hot, earthy broth with soft noodles and tender chicken or thinly sliced beef, and it is often served with other meaty additions, such as brisket, tripe, heart and other organs. Pho is a dish that celebrates true nose-to-tail eating.

The style and flavour of pho varies from region to region. In the north, the broth is light and delicate with lots of ginger, and the condiments include pickled onion, blanched bean sprouts and sliced chillies in fish sauce. In the south, the broth is richer and deeper in spices and served with more condiments, while in central Vietnam, the broth is also quite light, but is flavoured with chilli and lemongrass. Condiments here include salad leaves, pickles, chilli and garlic.

The pho I serve at Pho Nom is a recipe passed down from my mother. The recipe uses brisket and oxtail to extract a flavoursome beef broth with heady spices and no MSG. The stock relies on good-quality beef bones and is reduced over a long period, to develop maximum flavour.

# BÚN RIÊU
Crab noodle soup

My wife absolutely loves this soup, and it's always a hit when I make it at home. Don't be put off by the length of the recipe – the results are fantastic, and I promise that you'll keep coming back for more.

200 g (7 oz) pig's blood (available from Asian butchers), cut into 3 cm (1¼ in) cubes
250 g (9 oz) packet fried tofu, cubed
4 ripe tomatoes, halved
450 g (1 lb) thin bun (rice noodles)
1 bunch spring onions (scallions), thinly sliced, to serve
1 bunch coriander (cilantro), leaves picked, to serve

**Broth**
1 kg (2 lb 3 oz) pork bones (shin bones have the best flavour)
2 kg (4 lb 6 oz) chicken bones
1 kg (2 lb 3 oz) pork hock, cut into 8 rounds about 3 cm (1¼ in) thick (ask your butcher to do this for you)
300 ml (10 fl oz) fish sauce
100 g (3½ oz) caster (superfine) sugar
2 tablespoons sea salt

**Crab mousse**
1 tablespoon vegetable oil
2 garlic cloves, minced
2 shallots, minced
200 g (7 oz) jar crab paste with soya bean oil (see note)
70 g (2½ oz) dried shrimp, rehydrated for at least 2 hours, drained and minced
500 g (1 lb 2 oz) minced (ground) pork
2 eggs
250 g (9 oz) fresh crab meat
1 tablespoon fish sauce
2 teaspoons caster (superfine) sugar

**Salad**
500 g (1 lb 2 oz) morning glory (water spinach)
1 kg (2 lb 3 oz) bean sprouts
1 bunch mint, leaves picked (optional)
1 bunch shiso leaves
shrimp paste, to serve (optional)

**1** To make the broth, rinse the pork and chicken bones and hock under cold running water to remove any blood or splinters. Transfer to a 10 litre (2½ gallon) stockpot, cover with cold water and bring to the boil for 10 minutes. Drain and rinse the bones and hock of any residual blood and impurities. Return the bones to a clean stockpot, cover with water to nearly the top of the pot and bring to the boil again, removing any impurities that rise to the surface. Add the hock, reduce the heat to a slow simmer and cook for 45 minutes or until the hock is soft and tender. Remove the hock and set aside to cool. Continue to simmer the stock for a further 3–4 hours, until the liquid has reduced by 20–30 per cent. Season with the fish sauce, sugar and salt, then strain the stock into a clean saucepan and discard the bones.

**2** To make the crab mousse, heat the oil in a frying pan over medium heat. Add the garlic and shallot and cook for 2–3 minutes, until fragrant. Add the crab paste and dried shrimp and cook for 5 minutes. Set aside to cool. Combine the pork mince, eggs, crab meat and cooled shrimp mixture in a bowl and season with the fish sauce and sugar.

**3** To make the salad, pick the morning glory leaves and save for another use. Use a morning glory shredder (see page 16) to shred the stems into thin curls. If you don't have access to a shredder, you can julienne the morning story glory stems instead. Soak the shredded stems in cold water until ready to serve, then drain and transfer to a serving bowl.

**4** Arrange the remaining salad ingredients except the shrimp paste in serving bowls or on a serving platter.

**5** Bring a saucepan of water to the boil, add the pig's blood and boil for 10 minutes. Remove and plunge into iced water. Drain when cool and set aside.

**6** To cook the crab mousse, bring the stock to a rolling simmer. Working in batches, spoon golf ball–sized balls of the crab mousse into the stock (about 6–8 balls at a time) and cook until the crab mousse balls rise to the top. Continue to cook for a further 5 minutes, then remove using a slotted spoon.

**7** Add the tofu and tomato to the stock and cook over low heat for 10 minutes.

**8** Cook the noodles according to the packet instructions, then drain and run under cold water until cool. Drain again and set aside.

**9** Divide the noodles among eight shallow bowls and evenly ladle the stock, tomato and tofu over the top. Add the crab mousse, pig's blood and hock and garnish with spring onion and coriander.

**10** Place the salad in the centre of the table, along with small bowls of shrimp paste (if using) for people to add to their soups. Dig in.

**Note:** Crab paste with soya bean oil can be purchased from Asian supermarkets.

# HỦ TIẾU NAM VANG

Phnom Penh noodle soup

My parents used to own a restaurant in Phnom Penh, that only served this dish. It originated from the city and 'nam vang' actually means Phnom Penh. It has since made its way to Vietnam, but I believe my mum still makes the best version – this recipe is how she taught me to make it.

---

1 kg (2 lb 3 oz) calamari hoods, cleaned and scored
16 green prawns (shrimp), peeled and deveined, tails
   left intact
300 g (10½ oz) pork liver
500 g (1 lb 2 oz) minced (ground) pork
400 g (14 oz) thin stick bun (rice noodles)
160 ml (5½ fl oz) Garlic oil (see page 212)
1 bunch spring onions (scallions), thinly sliced,
   to garnish
1 bunch coriander (cilantro), leaves picked, to garnish
2 tablespoons ground white pepper, to garnish
4 tablespoons minced salted radish (see note),
   to garnish

**Broth**
2 kg (4 lb 6 oz) pork bones
3 kg (6 lb 10 oz) chicken bones
1 kg (2 lb 3 oz) pork loin
2 whole dried squid (see note), rinsed
40 g (1½ oz) dried shrimp
1 daikon (white radish)
3 whole salted radish (see note)
1 garlic bulb, halved
60 g (2 oz) sea salt
300 ml (10 fl oz) fish sauce
150 g (5 oz) caster (superfine) sugar

**To serve**
1 kg (2 lb 3 oz) bean sprouts
4 bird's eye chillies, sliced
soy sauce, to serve
lemons wedges, to serve (optional)

**1**  To make the broth, rinse the pork and chicken bones under cold running water to remove any blood or splinters. Transfer to a 10 litre (2½ gallon) stockpot, cover with cold water and bring to the boil for 10 minutes, then drain the liquid and rinse the bones of any residual blood and impurities. Return the bones to a clean stockpot and add the pork loin. Cover with water to nearly the top of the pot and bring to the boil again, removing any impurities that rise to the surface.

**2**  Add the dried squid, dried shrimp, daikon, salted radish and garlic, and simmer for 45 minutes or until the pork loin is cooked through. Transfer the loin to a bowl of iced water and set aside for 10 minutes, then drain and thinly slice.

**3**  Continue to simmer the broth for 4–5 hours until reduced by 20 per cent. Season with the salt, fish sauce and sugar, then strain into a clean saucepan and discard the solids. Keep the broth warm over low heat.

**4**  Meanwhile, bring a saucepan of water to the boil, add the calamari and prawns and cook for 3 minutes, or until just cooked through. Using a slotted spoon, remove the calamari and prawns and immediately plunge into iced water. Drain and set aside.

**5**  Return the water to the boil, add the pork liver and cook for about 15 minutes, or until just cooked through. Drain and plunge the liver into iced water, then drain again and slice into thin pieces.

**6**  Place the minced pork in a frying pan over medium–high heat and pour in a ladle of the stock to loosen the mince. Cook for 5 minutes or until the minced is cooked through. Set aside.

**7**  Bring another saucepan of water to the boil. Divide the noodles into individual serves and, using a noodle basket if you have one, cook one serve at a time according to the packet instructions. Alternatively, cook the noodles together, then drain and quickly divide among serving bowls. Drizzle a little of the garlic oil over the noodles, so they don't stick together. Top with the prawns, calamari, pork liver, pork loin and minced pork. Ladle over the broth and garnish with the spring onion, coriander, pepper, salted radish and the remaining garlic oil.

**8**  Serve immediately with the bean sprouts, sliced chilli, soy sauce and lemon wedges (if using), and invite guests to add the condiments to their own soup.

**Note:** Salted radish and dried squid can be purchased online or from most Asian supermarkets.

# BÚN BÒ HUẾ

Spicy beef noodle soup

So spicy! But so great. This famous noodle soup from the Hue region packs a real flavour punch with the addition of lots of lemongrass and chilli. It always makes me get my sweat on!

━━━━━━━━━━━━━━━

200 g (7 oz) pig's blood (available from Asian butchers), cut into 3 cm (1¼ in) cubes
400 g (14 oz) thick bun (rice noodles)
200 g (7 oz) cha lua (Vietnamese ham), sliced
1 bunch spring onions (scallions), thinly sliced, to garnish
1 red onion, peeled and thinly sliced, to garnish
1 bunch coriander (cilantro), leaves picked, to garnish
4 long red chillies, sliced
4 lemons, cut into wedges (optional)

### Broth
5 kg (11 lb) beef shin bones
1 kg (2 lb 3 oz) pork hock, cut into 8–10 rounds about 3 cm (1¼ in) thick (ask your butcher to do this for you)
2 kg (4 lb 6 oz) gravy beef or stewing steak
200 g (7 oz) pineapple, peeled and cored, chopped into large chunks
4 lemongrass stalks, white part only, bruised
2 brown onions, peeled
3 tablespoons sea salt
200 ml (7 fl oz) fish sauce
100 g (3½ oz) caster (superfine) sugar

### Chilli sate
160 ml (5½ fl oz) Annatto oil (see page 214)
3 shallots, minced
2 lemongrass stalks, minced
4 garlic cloves, minced
4 bird's eye chillies, minced
3 tablespoons shrimp paste
2 tablespoons fish sauce
2 tablespoons caster (superfine) sugar
30 g (1 oz) chilli flakes

### Banana blossom salad
1 lemon
1 banana blossom
500 g (1 lb 2 oz) bean sprouts
1 bunch Thai basil, leaves picked
1 bunch shiso, leaves picked
100 g (3½ oz) shredded morning glory stems (see page 16)

**1** To make the broth, rinse the beef bones and hock under cold running water to remove any blood or splinters. Transfer to a 10 litre (2½ gallon) stockpot along with the gravy beef, cover with cold water and bring to the boil for 10 minutes. Drain and rinse the bones and hock of any residual blood and impurities. Return the bones, hock and beef to a clean stockpot, cover with water to nearly the top of the pot and bring to the boil again, removing any impurities that rise to the surface. Reduce the heat and simmer for 45 minutes until the hock is soft and cooked through. Remove from the broth, plunge into iced water, then drain and set aside.

**2** Add the pineapple, lemongrass and onion to the broth and cook for a further 2 hours until the beef is tender. Carefully remove the beef, plunge into iced water and drain. Thinly slice and set aside.

**3** Continue to simmer the broth for a further 3 hours or until reduced by 30 per cent. Season with the salt, fish sauce and sugar, then strain into a clean saucepan and discard the bones. Keep warm over low heat.

**4** Meanwhile, to make the chilli sate, place the annatto oil in a saucepan along with the shallot, lemongrass, garlic and chilli. Place over medium heat and cook for 3–4 minutes until soft and aromatic. Add the shrimp paste, fish sauce, sugar and chilli flakes and cook, stirring frequently, for 4–5 minutes until aromatic. Set aside.

**5** Bring a saucepan of water to the boil, add the pig's blood and boil for 10 minutes. Remove and plunge into iced water. Drain when cool and set aside.

**6** To prepare the salad, fill a non-reactive bowl with cold water and squeeze in the lemon. Peel and discard the outer layers and flowers of the banana blossom until you reach the light-coloured interior. Cut the blossom in half lengthways and remove the inner flowers. Thinly slice the blossom and immediately plunge into the lemon water. Set aside for 30 minutes, then drain and transfer to a serving bowl. Add the remaining salad ingredients and toss to combine.

**7** Return the broth to the boil and add the hock and chilli sate.

**8** Cook the noodles according to the packet instructions, then drain and divide among serving bowls. Top with the gravy beef, pork hock, chu lua and pig's blood. Ladle over the broth and garnish with spring onion, red onion and coriander. Place the salad, sliced chilli and lemon wedges (if using) in the centre of the table and invite guests to help themselves.

# MÌ SỦI CẢO

Prawn dumplings with egg noodles

This is a really simple recipe that I always make in large batches and freeze in individual portions along with the dumplings. It makes a fantastic quick dinner when I get home late from work and am starving hungry. Just heat it up, cook some noodles and you're good to go.

---

2 tablespoons vegetable oil
8–10 serves fresh thin egg noodles (each bundle is one serve)
80 ml (2½ fl oz/⅓ cup) Garlic oil (see page 212)
300 g (10½ oz) barbecued pork (purchased from Chinese barbecue shops), sliced
1 bunch Chinese celery, leaves roughly chopped, to garnish

**Broth**

5 kg (11 lb) chicken bones
1 daikon (white radish)
2 brown onions, peeled
1 garlic bulb, halved
60 g (2 oz) sea salt
150 g (5½ oz) caster (superfine) sugar
200 ml (7 fl oz) fish sauce

**Sui cao**

500 g (1 lb 2 oz) green prawns (shrimp), peeled and deveined
2 spring onions (scallions), thinly sliced
50 g (1¾ oz) wood ear mushrooms, minced
1 shallot, minced
1 garlic clove, minced
pinch of ground white pepper
2 tablespoons fish sauce
1 tablespoon caster (superfine) sugar
200 g (7 oz) packet wonton wrappers

**To serve**

500 g (1 lb 2 oz) bean sprouts
4 long red chillies, sliced
2 lemons, cut into wedges
soy sauce

**1**  To make the broth, rinse the chicken bones to remove any blood or splinters. Transfer the bones to a large stockpot and cover with 8 litres (2 gallons) cold water. Bring to the boil, skimming off any impurities that rise to the surface. Add the daikon, onion and garlic, then reduce the heat and simmer for 2 hours.

**2**  Meanwhile, make the sui cao. Using a knife, roughly mash the prawn meat. Transfer to a large bowl and add the spring onion, wood ear mushroom, shallot, garlic and white pepper. Mix well and season with the fish sauce and sugar.

**3**  To wrap the sui cao, place 1 teaspoon of the prawn mixture in the centre of a wonton skin. Moisten the edges with a little water and fold diagonally in half into a triangle. Push out any air that may be trapped in the dumpling. Dab the corners with a little more water, then bring the corners round to meet each other and firmly seal. Repeat until you've used all the filling and wonton wrappers.

**4**  When the broth is ready, season with the salt, sugar and fish sauce. Strain into a clean saucepan and discard the solids. Keep warm over low heat.

**5**  Bring a medium saucepan of water to the boil. Add the sui cao in small batches and cook for 5 minutes. Using a slotted spoon, remove the cooked dumplings to a plate and lightly drizzle with the vegetable oil to prevent them sticking.

**6**  In the same pan of boiling water, cook one roll of noodles at a time. Using tongs, move the noodles around to release the starch. Remove after 1 minute and run under cold water, then return to the boiling water for 15 seconds, strain again and transfer to a serving bowl. Lightly drizzle with garlic oil, then repeat with the remaining noodles and garlic oil.

**7**  Assemble the barbecued pork and sui cao on top of the noodles. Ladle over the broth and garnish with the celery leaves. Serve with the bean sprouts, sliced chilli, lemon wedges and soy sauce on the table for guests to help themselves.

# BÁNH CANH CUA

## Crab and thick rice noodles

Traditionally this soup uses mud crab, but I much prefer blue swimmer crab as the shells are easier to remove and I find the meat tastes sweeter. My mother, however, is a traditionalist and swears by mud crab. Try it both ways and see which way – traditional or modern – you think is best!

---

8 whole blue swimmer or 4 whole mud crabs, cleaned
1.2 kg (2 lb 10 oz) fresh banh canh (tapioca noodles) (see note)
2 tablespoons ground white pepper
1 bunch spring onions (scallions), thinly sliced, to garnish
2 long red chillies, sliced
4 lemons, cut into wedges

### Broth

2 kg (4 lb 6 oz) chicken bones
1 kg (2 lb 3 oz) pork ribs, cut into 5 cm (2 in) lengths (ask your butcher to do this for you)
2 brown onions, peeled
1 garlic bulb, halved
300 ml (10 fl oz) fish sauce
200 g (7 oz) caster (superfine) sugar
100 g (3½ oz) cornflour (corn starch)

### Crab mix

80 ml (2½ fl oz/⅓ cup) Annatto oil (see page 214)
2 garlic cloves, minced
3 shallots, minced
300 g (10½ oz) fresh crab meat
2 tablespoons fish sauce
1 tablespoon caster (superfine) sugar

**1** To make the broth, rinse the chicken bones and pork ribs under cold running water to remove any blood or splinters. Transfer to a 10 litre (2½ gallon) stockpot, cover with cold water and bring to the boil for 10 minutes, then drain and rinse the bones and ribs of any residual blood and impurities. Return the bones and ribs to a clean stockpot, cover with water to nearly the top of the pot and bring to the boil again, removing any impurities that rise to the surface. Reduce the heat and simmer for 1 hour, then add the onion and garlic. Continue to simmer for a further 2 hours or until the broth has reduced by 30 per cent.

**2** To make the crab mix, heat the annatto oil in a saucepan over medium heat. Add the garlic and shallot and cook for 5–7 minutes until soft. Add the crab meat, stir to combine and season with the fish sauce and sugar. Cook for a further 5 minutes, then remove from the heat and set aside.

**3** Set up a large bamboo steamer over a saucepan of simmering water. Working in batches, if necessary, place the crabs on a plate, then transfer to the steamer, cover and steam for 10 minutes or until cooked through. Carefully remove the crabs, then strain the liquid on the plate through a fine sieve into the crab mix. Stir to combine.

**4** When the broth is ready, strain into a clean saucepan and discard the chicken bones. Return the pork ribs to the broth, add the crab mix and season with the fish sauce and sugar.

**5** Combine the cornflour and 100 ml (3½ fl oz) water, then slowly add to the broth to thicken, stirring constantly so it doesn't get lumpy.

**6** Blanch the banh canh noodles in a saucepan of boiling water for 3–4 minutes, then drain and divide among serving bowls. Ladle over the broth and pork ribs and top with a crab (or half a crab if using mud crabs). Garnish with the spring onion and serve with the sliced chilli and lemon wedges on the side.

**Note:** Fresh banh canh noodles can be purchased from Asian supermarkets.

# CHÁO GÀ

Chicken congee

Chicken congee is our go-to staff meal at Annam over the winter months. It's warm, comforting and filling, and super easy to make.

---

200 g (7 oz/1 cup) jasmine rice
2 tablespoons sea salt
1 tablespoon caster (superfine) sugar
ground white pepper, to garnish
1 bunch spring onions (scallions), thinly sliced, to garnish

**Chicken broth**
1 kg (2 lb 3 oz) chicken bones
1 × 1 kg (2 lb 3 oz) free-range chicken
1 onion, peeled
2 garlic cloves

**To serve**
1 lemon, cut into wedges
4 bird's eye chillies, sliced (optional)
1 kg (2 lb 3 oz) bean sprouts
3 tablespoons Fried shallots (see page 212)
Maggi seasoning

**1**  To make the broth, rinse the chicken bones to remove any blood and splinters. Transfer to a large stockpot, add the chicken and cover with 3 litres (3 qts) water. Bring to the boil, skimming off any impurities that rise to the top, then reduce the heat to a simmer, add the onion and garlic and cook for 30 minutes. Remove the chicken from the broth and set aside to cool. Strain the broth and discard the solids.

**2**  Place the rice and 2 litres (2 qts) of the chicken broth in a saucepan. Bring to the boil and cook for 40 minutes or until the rice is fully cooked. The broth should be thick from the rice and resemble a porridge. Season with the salt and sugar.

**3**  Tear the meat from the chicken and add to the rice porridge. Discard the bones.

**4**  To serve, ladle the congee into bowls and garnish with the pepper and spring onion. Serve with lemon wedges, sliced chilli (if using), bean sprouts and Maggi seasoning in the centre of the table for people to add to their own congee.

# LẦU

Hotpot

Hotpot is one of the most popular ways to eat for Vietnamese people. You might think a dish like this would be unpopular in such a hot country, but it's versatility and simplicity make it a favourite for many. The broth can be adapted to your liking, and you can use whichever ingredients are in season.

A hotpot is always placed in the centre of the table with a wide variety of ingredients for people to choose and then cook in the soup. The dish is normally shared among large groups of people, slowly grazing through the food while talking away and guzzling bia (beer).

Hotpot is my favourite dish. I like cooking food as I go, and the combination of noodles, soup, meat and vegetables means that I get a little bit of everything that I love!

---

2 litres (2 qts) Chicken broth (see page 146)
2 teaspoons sea salt
2 teaspoons caster (superfine) sugar
small handful coriander (cilantro) leaves
3 spring onions (scallions), thinly sliced
500 g (1 lb 2 oz) dried instant egg noodles

**Vegetables**
200 g (7 oz) shimeji mushrooms, separated
  into clumps
200 g (7 oz) oyster mushrooms
200 g (7 oz) morning glory (water spinach)
2 bunches bok choy, quartered

**Meat and seafood**
200 g (7 oz) calamari hoods and tentacles, cleaned
  and hoods scored (optional)
12 green prawns (shrimp), peeled and deveined
4 cooked blue swimmer crabs
300 g (10½ oz) sirloin beef (preferably wagyu),
  very thinly sliced
12 fish balls (see note)
12 beef balls (see note)
6 fish cakes (see note)

**Dipping sauce**
125 ml (4 fl oz/½ cup) hoi sin sauce
80 g (2¾ oz) satay sauce (store-bought is fine)
1 tablespoon sriracha chilli sauce
juice of 1 lime

**1** For this recipe, you will need a portable gas stove that can sit in the centre of your table. You can buy these at Asian kitchenware or camping stores.

**2** Combine the dipping sauce ingredients in a large bowl, then divide among individual ramekins for dipping.

**3** Place the stove on the table. Pour the chicken broth into a large hotpot and place the hotpot on the stove over medium heat. Season with the salt and sugar and add the coriander and spring onion.

**4** Place the raw ingredients in bowls or on plates, keeping the meat and seafood separate, and distribute around the table.

**5** Wait until the broth comes to the boil, then invite guests to select and cook their own ingredients.

The following are approximate cooking times for each ingredient, depending on their size:

– Dried instant egg noodles: 5–8 minutes
– Mushrooms: 5–7 minutes
– Morning glory and bok choy: 3–7 minutes
– Calamari: 4–5 minutes
– Prawns: 3–5 minutes
– Blue swimmer crabs: just heat through
– Sirloin beef: 1 minute
– Fish balls, beef balls and fish cakes: just heat
  through

**Note:** Fish balls, beef balls and fish cakes can be purchased from Asian supermarkets.

HOW TO EAT PHO

One of the best things about pho is that it can be altered to suit your own taste. Love chilli? Go crazy and spice it up. Got a sweet tooth? No problem – add a little hoi sin sauce.

Keep these tips in mind when eating your pho, and you'll be sure to enjoy a bowl that is uniquely yours.

### STEP 1 – TASTE THE BROTH

All phos are different, so before you start adding things, taste the broth you've got in front of you. Get an understanding of the flavours in your bowl and think about what you want to add to make it perfect.

### STEP 2 – SEASON YOUR PHO

So much about pho is getting the balance right. The condiments I like to have available are fresh lemon for sourness, fish sauce for a salty kick, hoi sin sauce to make it sweet and sriracha chilli sauce for spice. Know what you like and go for it, adding a little at a time and tasting as you go to make sure it's just right. (Insider tip: I like to make a dipping sauce by mixing Lemongrass sate (see page 206), hoi sin sauce and sriracha, to create my own condiment that is brilliant for dipping proteins into.)

### STEP 3 – FRESHEN IT UP!

This step is about the herbs you can add to enhance your pho. All phos need bean sprouts – how many is up to you. Add a small amount of bean sprouts at a time, otherwise they will lower the temperature of the stock. I always add Thai basil and recommend a little fresh chilli to make the soup taste really fresh.

### STEP 4 – MIX AND ENJOY!

Use your chopsticks to mix everything together and slurp away!

# PHỞ BÒ
## Beef pho

Pho bo is my absolute favourite pho. It has a rich beef flavour and fat from the top of the broth, which is referred to as the golden layer. It's this fat that gives beef pho its unique aroma.

---

2 kg (4 lb 6 oz) fresh pho noodles (see note)
1 kg (2 lb 3 oz) beef blade steak, very thinly sliced
1 brown onion, thinly sliced
1 bunch spring onions (scallions), thinly sliced
1 bunch coriander (cilantro), leaves picked

### Broth
5 kg (11 lb) beef marrowbones
200 g (7 oz) piece of ginger, unpeeled
2 large brown onions, unpeeled
1 garlic bulb, unpeeled, halved
1 × 500 g (1 lb 2 oz) beef brisket
1 kg (2 lb 3 oz) oxtail
15 star anise
2 black cardamom pods
2 sticks cassia bark
4 cloves
1 tablespoon coriander seeds
60 g (2 oz) sea salt
200 ml (7 fl oz) fish sauce
50 g (1¾ oz) caster (superfine) sugar (if needed)

### Accompaniments
1 kg (2 lb 3 oz) bean sprouts
2 bunches Thai basil
2 lemons, cut into wedges
6 bird's eye chillies, sliced
hoi sin sauce
sriracha chilli sauce
fish sauce

**1**   To make the broth, rinse the marrowbones to remove any blood and splinters, then transfer to a 10 litre (2½ gallon) stockpot. Fill the pot with enough cold water to cover the bones, then place over high heat and bring to the boil. Boil the bones for 20–30 minutes, until no more blood comes to the surface. Drain and discard the cooking liquid, and rinse any remaining blood or impurities from the bones. Return the bones to a clean stockpot, cover with water to nearly the top of the pot and bring back to the boil.

**2**   Meanwhile, roast the ginger, onion and garlic over a gas stovetop or barbecue flame, or under the grill (broiler) until the skins are charred. Add to the stockpot, along with the brisket and oxtail. Simmer for about 3 hours, removing any impurities as they rise to the surface, or until the meat is tender. Remove the brisket from the broth and set aside to cool, then place in the fridge to use later in the soup. Leave the oxtail in the broth.

**3**   Bring the stock back to the boil and continue to remove any impurities that rise to the surface. Simmer gently over medium heat for a further 7–8 hours until the broth has reduced by 20–30 per cent.

**4**   After 5–6 hours of cooking, lightly toast the star anise, cardamom pods, cassia bark, cloves and coriander seeds in a dry frying pan over medium heat until fragrant. Tie the spices in a square of muslin (cheesecloth) and add to the stockpot for the last few hours of cooking.

**5**   When the broth is ready, remove and discard the solids. Strain the broth through a fine sieve into a clean saucepan. Season the broth with the salt and fish sauce, and add the sugar if you feel the broth needs a little sweetness. Return to a low heat and simmer until ready to serve.

**6**   Bring a large saucepan of water to the boil. Using a noodle basket (see note), blanch individual portions of pho noodles (about 120 g–150 g/4 oz–5½ oz per person) for 10 seconds, then transfer to large noodle bowls.

**7**   Slice the brisket into 2 mm (¹⁄₁₆ in) thick slices and evenly divide among the bowls. Top with the thinly sliced beef blade, onion, spring onion and coriander. Ladle the stock into the bowls, ensuring that it's boiling hot to cook the raw beef slices.

**8**   Place the accompaniments on a serving platter and place in the centre of the table. Serve the pho and invite guests to season and flavour their own dish.

**Notes:** Fresh pho noodles can be purchased from most Asian supermarkets. If you are unable to find them, you can also use dried thin rice stick noodles (sometimes referred to as pad thai noodles). Cook according to the packet instructions, then drain and divide among noodle bowls.

It's best to use an Asian noodle-blanching basket to cook the noodles. These can be purchased from Asian kitchen supply stores or online.

# PHỞ GÀ

Chicken pho

For the uninitiated, this is a great entry-level pho. Pho ga has a delicate and light-tasting broth that contrasts wonderfully with the bold-tasting flavours of the accompaniments.

2 kg (4 lb 6 oz) fresh pho noodles (see note)
1 brown onion, thinly sliced
1 bunch spring onions (scallion), thinly sliced
1 bunch coriander (cilantro), leaves picked

**Broth**
3 kg (6 lb 10 oz) chicken bones
1 old hen or stewing bird (optional)
200 g (7 oz) piece of ginger, unpeeled
2 large brown onions, unpeeled
1 garlic bulb, unpeeled, halved
1 × 1 kg (2 lb 3 oz) free-range chicken
6 star anise
2 black cardamom pods
1 small stick cassia bark
50 g (1¾ oz) coriander seeds
3 tablespoons sea salt
200 ml (7 fl oz) fish sauce
50 g (1¾ oz) caster (superfine) sugar

**Accompaniments**
1 kg (2 lb 3 oz) bean sprouts
2 bunches Thai basil
6 bird's eye chillies, sliced
3 lemons, cut into wedges
sriracha chilli sauce
hoi sin sauce
Lemongrass sate (see page 206)
fish sauce

**1**  To make the broth, rinse the chicken bones to remove any blood and splinters, then transfer to a 10 litre (2½ gallon) stockpot. Fill the pot with enough cold water to cover the bones, then place over high heat and bring to the boil. Boil the bones for 20–30 minutes, until no more blood comes to the surface. Drain and discard the cooking liquid, and rinse any remaining blood or impurities from the bones. Return the bones to a clean stockpot and add the old hen (if using). Cover with water to nearly the top of the pot and bring back to the boil.

**2**  Meanwhile, roast the ginger, onion and garlic over a gas stovetop or barbecue flame, or under the grill (broiler) until the skins are blistered and aromatic. Rinse off any burnt bits and add, whole, to the broth, along with the whole chicken. Poach the chicken for 15–20 minutes until cooked through, then remove from the broth and set aside to cool.

**3**  Remove the chicken meat from the bones and return the bones to the broth. Tear the chicken meat into smaller pieces and set aside.

**4**  Toast the star anise, cardamom pods, cassia bark and coriander seeds in a dry frying pan over medium heat until fragrant. Tie the spices in a square of muslin (cheesecloth) and drop it into the broth. Continue to gently simmer the broth over medium heat for a further 4–5 hours until the broth has reduced by 20–30 per cent.

**5**  When the stock is ready, remove and discard the bones, old hen and spices. Strain the stock through a fine sieve into a clean saucepan. Season the stock with the salt, fish sauce and sugar. Return to a low heat and simmer until ready to serve.

**6**  Bring a large saucepan of water to the boil. Blanch individual portions (see note) of the pho noodles (about 120 g–150 g/4 oz–5½ oz per person) for 10 seconds, then transfer to large noodle bowls. Evenly divide the chicken among the bowls, pour over the hot stock and top with the onion, spring onion and coriander.

**7**  Place the accompaniments on a serving platter and place in the centre of the table. Serve the pho and invite guests to season and flavour their own dish.

**Notes:** Fresh pho noodles can be purchased from most Asian supermarkets. If you are unable to find them, you can also use dried thin rice stick noodles (sometimes referred to as pad thai noodles). Cook according to the packet instructions, then drain and divide among noodle bowls.

It's best to use an Asian noodle-blanching basket to cook the noodles. These can be purchased from Asian kitchen supply stores or online.

# PHỞ CHAY

Mushroom and tofu pho

Pho chay is a great noodle soup option for those who don't eat meat. Feel free to add other veggies to the broth if you like, but root vegetables and cabbage tend to result in a more rounded flavour.

---

1 kg (2 lb 3 oz) fresh pho noodles (see note)
500 g (1 lb 2 oz) organic tofu, cut 2 cm (¾ in) cubes
200 g (7 oz) enoki mushrooms, separated into clumps
200 g (7 oz) oyster mushrooms
1 red onion, thinly sliced
1 bunch spring onions (scallions), thinly sliced
1 bunch coriander (cilantro), leaves picked

**Broth**
2 carrots
1 small wombok (Chinese cabbage)
½ white cabbage
250 g (9 oz) ginger, unpeeled
1 onion, unpeeled
1 garlic bulb, unpeeled, halved
4 star anise
1 black cardamom pod
1 small stick cassia bark
50 g (1¾ oz) coriander seeds
3 tablespoons salt, to taste
1 tablespoon caster (superfine) sugar, to taste

**Accompaniments**
500 g (1 lb 2 oz) bean sprouts
1 bunch Thai basil
5 bird's eye chillies, sliced
3 lemons, cut into wedges
hoi sin sauce

**1** To make the broth, place the carrots, wombok and cabbage in a 10 litre (2½ gallon) stockpot and cover with water to nearly the top of the pot. Place over high heat, bring to the boil and skim off any scum that rises to the surface. Reduce to a simmer.

**2** Meanwhile, roast the ginger, onion and garlic over a gas stovetop or barbecue flame, or under the grill (broiler) until the skins are blistered and aromatic. Rinse off any burnt bits and add, whole, to the broth.

**3** Toast the star anise, cardamom pod, cassia bark and coriander seeds in a dry frying pan over medium heat until fragrant. Tie the spices in a square of muslin (cheesecloth) and drop it into the broth. Continue to simmer the broth over medium heat for 3–4 hours until it has reduced by 20–30 per cent. Strain the broth into a clean saucepan and season with the salt and sugar. Return the broth to a simmer. Discard the solids.

**4** Bring a large saucepan of water to the boil. Blanch individual portions (see note) of the pho noodles (about 120 g–150 g/4 oz–5½ oz per person) for 10 seconds, then transfer to large noodle bowls. Evenly divide the tofu and mushrooms among the bowls, pour over the hot broth and top with the onion, spring onion and coriander.

**5** Place the accompaniments on a serving platter and place in the centre of the table. Serve the pho and invite guests to season and flavour their own dish.

**Notes:** Fresh pho noodles can be purchased from most Asian supermarkets. If you are unable to find them, you can also use dried thin rice stick noodles (sometimes referred to as pad thai noodles). Cook according to the packet instructions, then drain and divide among noodle bowls.

It's best to use an Asian noodle-blanching basket to cook the noodles. These can be purchased from Asian kitchen supply stores or online.

RICE
RICE RICE
RICE RICE
RICE RICE

Rice is a very important staple for Vietnamese people. Even though many graze on snacks and small dishes throughout the day, rice is often a large component at mealtimes. Office workers sustain themselves for lunch with affordable rice dishes – the Vietnamese version of fast food. These dishes are served as part of a large lunch, and although the options vary, the basics always include soup, meat and a vegetable to balance out the meal. Whenever I eat at home, this is how I eat.

# CƠM TẤM

Broken rice with pork chop

Com tam is a common lunchtime offering and has everything you could want on one plate. The broken rice is piled high with aromatic grilled pork chop, eggs, meatloaf and a small token salad. I love it! There is a great restaurant in Saigon that sells this dish, and I always make a stop there when I'm in town.

---

4 pork chops
400 g (14 oz/2 cups) jasmine rice
1 tablespoon vegetable oil
4 eggs
2 Lebanese (short) cucumbers, sliced on the angle
2 tomatoes, halved and sliced
100 g (3½ oz) Pickled carrot and daikon (see page 209)
80 ml (2½ fl oz/⅓ cup) Spring onion oil (see page 207)
250 ml (8½ fl oz/1 cup) Nuoc mam dipping sauce (see page 206)

## Marinade

3 tablespoons vegetable oil
pinch of ground white pepper
2 tablespoons finely chopped lemongrass (white part only)
2 tablespoons finely chopped garlic
2 tablespoons honey
100 ml (3½ fl oz) fish sauce
1 tablespoon caster (superfine) sugar
1 bird's eye chilli, finely chopped

## Pork loaf

2 eggs
500 g (1 lb 2 oz) minced (ground) pork
50 g (1¾ oz) wood ear mushrooms, roughly chopped
60 g (2 oz) glass (cellophane) noodles, rehydrated in cold water for 1 hour, drained and cut into short lengths
1 shallot, finely chopped
3 tablespoons fish sauce
1 tablespoon caster (superfine) sugar
pinch of ground white pepper

**1** First, marinate the pork chops. Combine the marinade ingredients in a large bowl. Tenderise the pork chops by lightly beating them with a meat mallet. Add to the marinade and mix well to coat the chops. Set aside for at least 3 hours or, preferably, overnight.

**2** To make the pork loaf, separate the eggs and set aside the yolks. Beat the egg whites in a large bowl until airy, then add the remaining ingredients, except the yolks, and mix well.

**3** Place a large bamboo steamer over a saucepan of boiling water. Line a 25 cm × 12 cm (10 in × 4¾ in) loaf (bar) tin with foil and spoon in the pork loaf mixture. Transfer the tin to the steamer and steam, covered, for 30 minutes. Open the lid and brush the reserved egg yolks on top of the loaf, then steam with the lid off for a further 5 minutes. Remove from the heat and set aside.

**4** Rinse the rice under cold water, then drain and transfer to a saucepan. Add enough water to just cover the rice (a rule of thumb is to measure the water with your index finger from the top of the rice to your first knuckle). Place the pan over medium–low heat and simmer until the water is absorbed and the rice is tender. Alternatively, cook the rice in a rice cooker.

**5** Prepare a charcoal grill or preheat a grill (broiler) to medium–high. When the charcoal grill is ready (the embers should be glowing red with a small flame on the charcoal) place the pork chops on the grill and cook, frequently turning and basting with the marinade, for 15 minutes or until cooked through.

**6** Heat the oil in a frying pan over medium–high heat. Crack the eggs into the pan and fry sunny side up. Allow the undersides of the eggs to get slightly crispy, then remove and rest on a plate lined with paper towel.

**7** To assemble, spoon the rice onto serving plates and arrange the cucumber, tomato, pickles and a thick slice of pork loaf around the edge. Top with a pork chop and fried egg and drizzle a little spring onion oil over the pork chop. Serve with nuoc mam on the side.

# GÀ XÀO GỪNG

Braised chicken in ginger

My father makes the best version of this. Dad rarely cooks, but when he does he does it so well. I remember standing on a stool by the stove as my father talked me through cooking this dish, the importance of infusing the ginger yourself and the fact that the chicken tastes better when it's still on the bone. I love to eat this meal with a bowl of fresh steamed jasmine rice. This is my comfort food!

---

1 × 1.8 kg (4 lb) chicken
2 tablespoons vegetable oil
150 g (5½ oz) ginger, peeled and julienned
50 g (1¾ oz) fine caster (superfine) sugar, plus extra if needed
80 ml (2½ fl oz/⅓ cup) fish sauce, plus extra if needed
1 teaspoon ground white pepper
2 long red chillies, sliced
handful coriander (cilantro) leaves
steamed jasmine rice, to serve

**1**  First, prepare the chicken. Using a cleaver or large knife, chop the chicken in half through the breastbone. Cut off the thighs, then break them down into 3–4 smaller pieces. Remove the chicken wings from the breast and cut off the tips. Finally, cut the breast into 5–6 pieces.

**2**  Place the oil and ginger in a large, deep frying pan with a lid and set over medium heat. Cook the ginger for 2–3 minutes until golden brown then, using a slotted spoon, remove the ginger from the oil and drain on a plate lined with paper towel. Set aside.

**3**  Add the sugar to the ginger-infused oil over low heat. Cook, stirring continuously, for 7–10 minutes until the mixture turns a golden caramel. Take care not to burn the caramel, otherwise the dish will be bitter.

**4**  Add the chicken to the pan and stir quickly and continuously to ensure the chicken and caramel don't stick to the bottom of the pan.

**5**  Reduce the heat to medium–low and add the ginger and fish sauce. Keep stirring the chicken to coat with the caramel, then cover and simmer for 30 minutes or until the chicken is cooked through. Check the seasoning and season with more sugar and fish sauce, if necessary.

**6**  Divide the chicken among serving bowls, sprinkle with white pepper and scatter the chilli and coriander over the top. Serve immediately with bowls of steamed rice.

# THỊT KHO

Caramelised pork belly

Thit kho is my winter warm-my-soul-up dish. It brings me such love and comfort, and brings back memories of when I was young and my mum would cook a large pot for the family during Tết Festival. My death-row meal would be a bowl of thit kho with a side of steamed rice.

---

1 kg (2 lb 3 oz) pork belly, cut into 3 cm (1¼ in) cubes
2 spring onions (scallions), white part only, lightly bruised
2 garlic cloves, crushed
200 ml (7 fl oz) fish sauce, plus extra if needed
150 g (5½ oz) caster (superfine) sugar, plus extra if needed
vegetable oil for frying and deep-frying
juice of 2 young coconuts
4 eggs
steamed jasmine rice, to serve

**Garnish**
spring onions (scallions), thinly sliced
pinch of ground white pepper

**1**   Bring a large saucepan of water to the boil, add the pork belly and blanch for 10–15 minutes. Drain the pork and rinse under cold running water. Set aside.

**2**   Combine the spring onion, garlic, 2 tablespoons of the fish sauce and 1 tablespoon of the sugar in a large bowl and stir until the sugar has dissolved. Add the pork and set aside in the fridge to marinate for at least 4 hours or, preferably, overnight.

**3**   Place 2 tablespoons of oil and the remaining sugar in a large saucepan over medium heat. Stir continuously for 4–6 minutes until the sugar caramelises and turns golden brown. Add the pork belly with its marinade and quickly stir through the caramel.

**4**   Add the remaining fish sauce and give everything a good stir. Add the coconut water and pour in enough cold water to just cover the pork. Simmer for 1–1½ hours until the meat is completely tender. Season to taste with more fish sauce and sugar, if necessary.

**5**   Meanwhile, to cook the eggs, bring a saucepan of water to the boil and gently lower in the eggs. Cook for 6½ minutes, so that the centres are still soft. Using a slotted spoon, remove the eggs from the pan and plunge into iced water. Peel and set aside.

**6**   Heat 1 litre (34 fl oz/4 cups) of vegetable oil in a large saucepan over medium–high heat to 180°C (350°F) on a kitchen thermometer. Carefully lower the eggs into the oil and deep-fry for 2–3 minutes until golden. Using a slotted spoon, remove the eggs and drain on a plate lined with paper towel.

**7**   To serve, divide the pork belly and cooking liquid among serving bowls. Cut the eggs in half and add to the bowls, and garnish with the spring onion and a pinch of white pepper. Serve with steamed rice.

# CÀ CHUA NHỒI THỊT
## Pork-stuffed tomatoes with dill

This dish is commonly found at 'office rice' venues in northern Vietnam. These venues serve a selection of affordable dishes to hungry office workers looking for something cheap and filling to sustain them through the afternoon.

This is one of my go-to office rice dishes. I love slathering the sauce over my rice!

---

6 large tomatoes
3 tablespoons vegetable oil
2 garlic cloves, crushed
3 shallots, thinly sliced
2 tablespoons fish sauce
1 tablespoon caster (superfine) sugar
1 sliced spring onion (scallion), to serve
2 dill sprigs, fronds picked, to serve
coriander (cilantro) leaves, to serve
steamed jasmine rice, to serve

### Pork filling
500 g (1 lb 2 oz) minced (ground) pork
1 shallot, minced
2 spring onions (scallions), thinly sliced
2 garlic cloves, minced
pinch of ground white pepper
3 wood ear mushrooms, chopped
50 g (1¾ oz) glass (cellophane) noodles, rehydrated in cold water for 1 hour, drained and cut into short lengths
2 tablespoons fish sauce
1 tablespoon caster (superfine) sugar

**1**  First, make the pork filling by combining all the ingredients in a bowl. Set aside.

**2**  Slice the tops off the tomatoes and scoop out the seeds and juice into a bowl. Set aside. Chop two of the tomatoes and add to the bowl with the seeds and juice.

**3**  Using a spoon, carefully fill the four remaining tomatoes with the pork filling mixture, pressing firmly to ensure the filling stays in the tomatoes.

**4**  Heat the oil in a large frying pan with a lid over medium–high heat and add the tomatoes, top side down. Cook for 7–10 minutes until browned. Remove from the pan and set aside on a plate.

**5**  Add the garlic and shallot to the pan and cook for 5 minutes, until soft. Add the reserved tomato seeds and juice and the two chopped tomatoes. Simmer over medium heat for 30 minutes, then season with the fish sauce and sugar. Return the stuffed tomatoes to the pan and simmer, covered, for 15 minutes or until the pork is cooked through (the tomatoes will be firm when gently squeezed).

**6**  Transfer the tomatoes and the sauce to a serving plate, sprinkle with the spring onion, dill and coriander and serve with steamed rice on the side.

# RAU MUỐNG XÀO TƯƠNG

Stir-fried morning glory

So simple, yet so good! Stir-fried morning glory is a fantastic healthy side dish, which is often served as part of an office rice meal. It's also served at big family meals as part of a shared feast.

---

2 tablespoons vegetable oil
2 garlic cloves, crushed
1 long red chilli, cut in half lengthways
500 g (1 lb 2 oz) morning glory (water spinach)
1 teaspoon fermented yellow soy beans (see note)

**1**  Heat a wok over high heat and add the vegetable oil. When the oil is smoking add the garlic, chilli and morning glory and toss together quickly.

**2**  Add 2 tablespoons water and the fermented soy beans. Toss the soy beans through evenly, then transfer to a serving plate and serve immediately.

**Note:** Fermented yellow soy beans can be purchased from most Asian supermarkets.

# CANH TÔM BỊ ĐAU

Melon and prawn soup

This soup is a perfect accompaniment to any of the rice dishes in this chapter. It's a light and delicate broth with sweetness from the melon and prawns. Soups are very commonly served alongside rice dishes in Vietnam, as they serve as a palate cleanser between the different flavours on the plate.

---

4 large green prawns (shrimp), peeled and deveined
2 tablespoons fish sauce, plus extra to taste
1 tablespoon caster (superfine) sugar, plus
    extra to taste
1 teaspoon ground white pepper, plus extra to garnish
2 spring onions (scallions), thinly sliced, plus extra
    to garnish
500 g (1 lb 2 oz) hairy (fuzzy) melon, peeled and cut
    into 2 cm (¾ in) cubes

**1**  Using a knife, lightly smash the prawns, then roughly chop them into chunks. Transfer to a bowl and add the fish sauce, sugar and pepper. Add the spring onion and mix thoroughly.

**2**  Bring 1.5 litres (1½ qts) water to the boil in a medium saucepan over medium heat. Add the melon and simmer for 20 minutes.

**3**  Gently add the prawn mixture to the soup and season to taste with fish sauce and sugar. Simmer for a further 15 minutes.

**4**  Divide the soup among bowls, making sure everyone gets an even amount of melon and prawn, and garnish with extra spring onion and pepper. Serve immediately.

# CƠM GÀ HỘI AN

Hoi An chicken rice

This is a very interesting dish that's rarely found outside of Hoi An. The style of cooking the chicken is very similar to the Chinese method of cooking Hainanese chicken, but the finished dish is closer to a chicken salad. It is traditionally served with fresh green papaya and earthy turmeric rice. I love it.

---

1 × 1.8 kg (4 lb) free-range chicken
1 tablespoon sea salt
1 tablespoon ground turmeric
400 g (14 oz/2 cups) jasmine rice
50 g (1¾ oz/¼ cup) white glutinous rice
Nuoc mam dipping sauce (see page 206), to serve

### Salad

200 g (7 oz) shredded green papaya
1 brown onion, thinly sliced
1 bunch Vietnamese mint, leaves picked
100 g (3½ oz) Pickled carrot and daikon (see page 209)

**1**  Rinse the chicken and pat dry with paper towel. Bring a large saucepan of water to the boil, add the chicken, salt and turmeric and poach the chicken for 15 minutes. Turn off the heat and leave the chicken in the liquid for a further 25 minutes, then remove the chicken and cool on a wire rack. Reserve the poaching liquid.

**2**  Combine the rice and glutinous rice and rinse under cold water for 2 minutes, moving the rice the whole time to ensure each grain is well rinsed. Drain and transfer the rice to a saucepan and pour in enough poaching liquid to cover the rice by about 2 cm (¾ in). Place over medium heat, bring to the boil, then reduce the heat to a simmer and cook for 15 minutes or until the liquid has been absorbed and the rice is tender.

**3**  Remove the chicken thighs from the chicken and chop into small pieces. Remove the breast meat from the bone and thickly slice. Place the thighs, chicken breast and wings on a serving platter.

**4**  Combine the salad ingredients in a bowl. Divide the nuoc mam among individual serving bowls.

**5**  To serve, spoon the rice onto plates, along with the salad. Invite guests to help themselves to the poached chicken and add their own nuoc mam.

ERTS
ERTS
ERTS
ERTS
ERTS

Desserts in Vietnam often take the form of sweet, cold drinks to be enjoyed as a relief from the heat. These are referred to as che, and consist of different kinds of beans, such as mung beans, red kidney beans, red beans or black beans. The beans are cooked in sugar syrup and served with different jellies, lots of coconut cream and an abundance of shaved ice. My favourites are che thai and che ba mau, both of which feature in this chapter. Other che are served warm, such as che troi nuoc (sticky mochi-like balls filled with mung beans in ginger syrup) and che bap (sweet corn pudding).

Other desserts are left over from French colonialism – flans and caramels that the Vietnamese converted to make their own. My favourite is the coffee caramel, which takes a standard caramel and flavours it with the best Vietnamese coffee. I have also added one of my favourite desserts to this chapter: fried ice cream! It's a dish that the first wave of Vietnamese immigrants brought to Australia and, to this day, it remains extremely popular.

# CHÈ THÁI

Vietnamese fruit cocktail

This Vietnamese version of the famous fruit cocktail provides the perfect sugar kick when you need a sweet pick-me-up!

---

565 g (1 lb 4 oz) tin jackfruit
565 g (1 lb 4 oz) tin longans
565 g (1 lb 4 oz) tin toddy palm
530 g (15 oz) tin grass jelly (ai-yu jelly), diced
500 ml (17 fl oz/2 cups) coconut cream
ice cubes or crushed ice, to serve

**Mock pomegranate seeds**
100 g (3½ oz) tin water chestnuts
few drops of red food colouring
100 g (3½ oz/1 cup) tapioca flour

**1**  To make the mock pomegranate seeds, dice the water chestnuts into small pieces to represent real pomegranate seeds. Place in a bowl and sprinkle with a few drops of red food colouring. Mix well to coat the diced chestnut and set aside for 30 minutes.

**2**  Bring a saucepan of water to the boil.

**3**  Place the tapioca flour in a bowl and toss through the red chestnut pieces. Remove any excess flour, then drop into the boiling water and cook until the chestnut floats to the top, about 2–3 minutes. Using a slotted spoon, remove the chestnut and plunge into iced water to stop the cooking process. Drain and set aside.

**4**  Strain the syrup from the fruit tins into a bowl. Roughly tear the jackfruit into bite-sized chunks.

**5**  Divide the fruit among glasses and pour over the fruit syrup. Top with the grass jelly and mock pomegranate seeds, then pour in the coconut cream. Top with ice and serve.

# CHÈ BA MÀU

Three colour che

'Three colour' desserts are a popular sweet street-food in Vietnam. They make the perfect end to a meal or after a hearty bowl of pho.

---

oil spray
500 ml (17 fl oz/2 cups) coconut cream
crushed ice or ice cubes, to serve

**Pandan jelly**
1 teaspoon pandan colouring (extract)
110 g (4 oz/½ cup) caster (superfine) sugar
2 tablespoons agar-agar powder

**Red beans**
400 g (14 oz) can red kidney beans
110 g (4 oz/½ cup) caster (superfine) sugar

**Mung beans**
200 g (7 oz) mung beans, soaked in cold
   water overnight
3 tablespoons caster (superfine) sugar

**1**   Spray a 20 cm x 5 cm x 5 cm loaf (bar tin) with oil spray.

**2**   To make the pandan jelly, combine the ingredients and 1 litre (34 fl oz/4 cups) water in a saucepan and whisk continuously over medium heat until the sugar has dissolved. Strain into the prepared tin and set aside in the fridge for at least 1 hour until set.

**3**   To make the red beans, combine the kidney beans and the water from the tin, the sugar and 250 ml (8½ fl oz/1 cup) water in a saucepan. Bring to the boil over medium heat, then simmer for 30 minutes. Set aside to cool.

**4**   Meanwhile, drain the mung beans and place in a saucepan with 300 ml (10 fl oz) water. Bring to the boil over medium heat and simmer for 20 minutes or until soft. Drain, then transfer to a bowl and stir in the sugar. Transfer the mixture to a blender and blitz to a smooth paste. Set aside.

**5**   Once the pandan jelly is set, flip it out onto a chopping board and, using a serrated knife, cut into 5 mm (¼ in) wide strips.

**6**   To assemble, layer the pandan jelly, red beans and mung beans in tall glasses. Drizzle over some coconut cream, top with ice and serve.

# KEM CHIÊN

Deep-fried ice cream with salted caramel

Vietnamese immigrants brought fried ice cream to Australia. Years ago when my brother was at school, he mentioned this delicious dessert in one of his assignments and the teacher laughed at him. 'You can't fry ice cream,' she proclaimed. Well, look who's laughing now!

You need to start this recipe two days ahead.

---

8 × 70 g (2½ oz) scoops salted caramel ice cream
500 g (1 lb 2 oz) waffles
150 g (5½ oz/1 cup) plain (all-purpose) flour
3 eggs, lightly beaten
2 litres (2 qts) vegetable oil, for deep-frying

**Salted caramel**
220 g (8 oz/1 cup) caster (superfine) sugar
90 g (3 oz) butter
140 ml (4½ fl oz) cream
1½ tablespoons sea salt

**1** Line a large baking tray with baking paper. Working quickly, place the ice cream scoops on the tray, then transfer to the freezer and freeze overnight.

**2** Working in batches, place the waffles in a food processor and blitz to a crumb. Set aside in a large shallow bowl.

**3** Place the flour in a separate shallow bowl and the beaten egg in a third bowl.

**4** Working quickly and with one ice cream ball at a time, roll the ice cream in the flour, making sure to dust off any excess, then roll through the egg wash. Transfer to the waffle crumb and roll until the ice cream is thickly coated. Firmly press the crumbs into the ice cream (this helps to protect the ice cream when it's fried). Return the ice cream balls to the freezer and freeze overnight.

**5** To make the salted caramel, place the sugar in a medium saucepan over medium heat and cook, stirring constantly, until the sugar has melted. As soon as the sugar has liquefied, stop stirring, as this will agitate it and cause the caramel to crystallise. Continue to cook until the sugar turns a deep caramel colour. Slowly whisk in the butter, followed by the cream, then remove from the heat and stir in the salt. Set aside.

**6** Heat the oil in a large saucepan to 200°C (400°F) on a kitchen thermometer. Working in batches, carefully lower the ice cream balls into the oil and cook for 30–40 seconds until golden brown. Using a slotted spoon, remove the ice cream from the oil and drain on a plate lined with paper towel.

**7** Serve in small bowls generously drizzled with the salted caramel.

# SỮA CHUA NẾP CẨM

Yoghurt with black sticky rice

I love the texture of black sticky rice; it retains a lovely chewy bite after cooking that contrasts beautifully with the silky yoghurt. Feel free to add any fresh fruit you like to this dish. Ripe mango is a firm Vietnamese favourite that works particularly well.

---

350 (12 oz) glutinous black rice, soaked
  in cold water overnight
2 pandan leaves
60 g (2 oz) grated palm sugar
pinch of sea salt
500 g (1 lb 2 oz/2 cups) Vietnamese yoghurt
  (see page 192)

**1**  Drain and rinse the rice, then place in a large saucepan with the pandan leaves and 1 litre (34 fl oz/4 cups) water. Set over medium–high heat and bring to the boil. Reduce the heat to a simmer and cook for 30 minutes, then stir through the palm sugar and salt and cook for a further 20 minutes, or until the rice is soft with a gentle bite and the water is absorbed. Transfer the rice to a bowl and set aside in the fridge until cool.

**2**  Spoon the sticky rice into tall glasses and top with the Vietnamese yoghurt. Serve.

# SỮA CHUA

Vietnamese yoghurt

People often ask me why Vietnamese yoghurt tastes so different. The answer? We use condensed milk! This not only makes the yoghurt a little sweeter, it also helps it to set more thickly.

395 g (13½ oz) tin condensed milk
60 g (2 oz/¼ cup) natural yoghurt
boiling water

**1**  Pour the condensed milk into a large bowl. Fill the condensed milk tin with hot water and add to the condensed milk. Add another tin of hot water followed by a tin of room temperature water. Whisk until well combined, then whisk in the yoghurt. Strain the mixture into 12 individual serving jars or one large glass jar. Seal.

**2**  Place the jars in a large saucepan and pour enough boiling water into the pan to come three-quarters of the way up the side of the jars. Cover and set aside for 8 hours or, preferably, overnight.

**3**  Remove the jars from the pan, and set aside in the fridge until set and completely chilled.

# CHUỐI CHIÊN DỪA

Coconut fried banana

This has to be one of my favourite desserts. I can eat platefuls of it, which is not always a good idea as it's quite rich. The contrasting textures are sublime, with the soft banana, crispy batter, refreshing ice cream and sweet salted caramel all coming together in the perfect mouthful. What's not to love?!

---

4 bananas
2 litres (2 qts) vegetable oil, for deep-frying
vanilla ice cream, to serve
Salted caramel (see page 189), to serve
shredded coconut, to serve

**Batter**
150 g (5½ oz/1 cup) plain (all-purpose) flour
90 g (3 oz) rice flour
15 g (½ oz/¼ cup) shredded coconut
1 tablespoon caster (superfine) sugar
pinch of salt
375 ml (12½ fl oz/1½ cups) soda water (club soda)
1 tablespoon sesame seeds

**1**  Whisk the batter ingredients in a large bowl until smooth. Set aside to rest for 20–30 minutes.

**2**  Peel the bananas and cut in half lengthways. Working with one half at a time, place a banana half between two pieces of plastic wrap and gently flatten the banana with the palm of your hand into a disc shape.

**3**  Dip the flattened banana halves in the batter, until thoroughly coated.

**4**  Heat the oil in a large saucepan over medium–high heat to 180°C (350°F) on a kitchen thermometer. Working in batches, deep-fry the bananas, turning every now and then, for 3–4 minutes until golden brown.

**5**  Serve with a scoop of vanilla ice cream, a good drizzle of salted caramel and a sprinkling of shredded coconut.

# CÀ PHÊ CARAMEL

Coffee caramel

**Serves 8**

This dish is a Vietnamese take on the classic French creme caramel. The coffee gives it a wonderful aroma. Try and use Vietnamese coffee if you can – Trung Nguyen coffee is an easy brand to find, or look out for Saigon coffee, which is what we use at Pho Nom and Annam. If you can't find Vietnamese coffee, then regular espresso is fine.

175 g (6 oz) caster (superfine) sugar, plus extra
  to serve
60 ml (2 fl oz/¼ cup) freshly brewed espresso
2 eggs
3 egg yolks
250 ml (8½ fl oz/1 cup) full-cream (whole) milk
340 ml (11½ fl oz/3 cups) pouring cream
2 teaspoons coffee beans, lightly crushed

1 Combine 100 g (3½ oz) of the sugar and 60 ml (2 fl oz/¼ cup) water in a saucepan and stir over low heat until the sugar has dissolved. Increase the heat to medium and boil, without stirring, for 10–15 minutes until the mixture turns golden and caramelises. Pour in the coffee, stir and simmer for 5 minutes. Carefully pour the coffee caramel into the base of eight 150 ml (5 fl oz) ramekins.

2 Preheat the oven to 120°C (240°F).

3 Whisk the eggs, egg yolks and the remaining sugar in a bowl.

4 Combine the milk, cream and crushed coffee beans in a saucepan and bring to a gentle simmer (do not let the mixture boil). Strain the mixture into a jug. Whisking the egg mixture continuously, slowly pour in the milk mixture. Divide the custard among the ramekins.

5 Place the ramekins in a baking dish and pour in enough hot water to come half way up the side of the ramekins. Bake for 40 minutes or until just set (the custards should be firm with just a little wobble).

6 Remove the ramekins from the dish and set aside in the fridge for at least 2 hours or, preferably, overnight.

7 To serve, run a knife around the edge of each ramekin and invert onto serving plates.

# COFFEE

Coffee culture is a large part of family life in Vietnam, and free time is often spent at coffee shops catching up with friends, playing chess or just watching the world go by.

Vietnam is the world's second largest producer of coffee. Most of the coffee is grown in the mountains of Da Lat, where they also make the world-famous civet coffee.

Vietnamese coffee percolators are cheap and can be easily found at most Asian supermarkets.

# CÀ PHÊ SỮA ĐÁ

**Serves 1**

Vietnamese iced coffee

condensed milk
2 teaspoons ground Vietnamese coffee
crushed ice, to serve

**1** Pour condensed milk into the bottom of a glass. Add as much or as little as you like, depending on your sweet tooth!

**2** Place a Vietnamese coffee percolator on top of the glass, spoon in the ground coffee and fill to the top with boiling water.

**3** When the coffee has finished dripping into the glass, remove the percolator. Vigorously stir the condensed milk and coffee to help air the drink, then top with ice and enjoy.

# SỮA CHUA CÀ PHÊ

Frozen yoghurt coffee

Serves 1

3 tablespoons Vietnamese yoghurt (see page 192)
2 teaspoons ground Vietnamese coffee
crushed ice, to serve

**1**  Freeze the yoghurt for 2–3 hours until frozen.

**2**  Place a Vietnamese coffee percolator on top of a glass, spoon in the ground coffee and fill to the top with boiling water.

**3**  When the coffee has finished dripping into the glass, remove the percolator. Half-fill with crushed ice and spoon the frozen yoghurt on top. Enjoy!

# CÀ PHÊ TRỨNG

Egg coffee

Serves 1

2 teaspoons ground Vietnamese coffee
2 egg yolks
3 tablespoons condensed milk

**1**  Place a coffee cup in a large bowl and pour hot water into the bowl (this will help to keep the coffee hot while it is brewing). Place a Vietnamese coffee percolator on top of the cup, spoon in the ground coffee and fill to the top with boiling water.

**2**  Vigorously whisk the egg yolks and condensed milk until light and fluffy.

**3**  When the coffee has finished dripping into the cup, remove the percolator and carefully spoon the egg mixture over the top.

**4**  To drink, either stir the sweetened egg mixture into the coffee or slowly eat with a spoon while sipping the black coffee underneath.

Vietnamese iced coffee

Frozen yoghurt coffee

Egg coffee

BAS
BAS
BAS

The recipes in this chapter will assist with many of the dishes in this book. These basics are at the core of Vietnamese cooking, and they all regularly make appearances in some form or another.

By familiarising yourself with the recipes that follow, you will equip yourself with an excellent understanding of the essence of Vietnamese flavours, plus they will help you identify all those unlabelled jars that adorn street-vendor carts when visiting Vietnam!

These are also the basics we teach our staff at Annam and Pho Nom. I recommend making large batches of these recipes, as most of them keep well and have multiple uses.

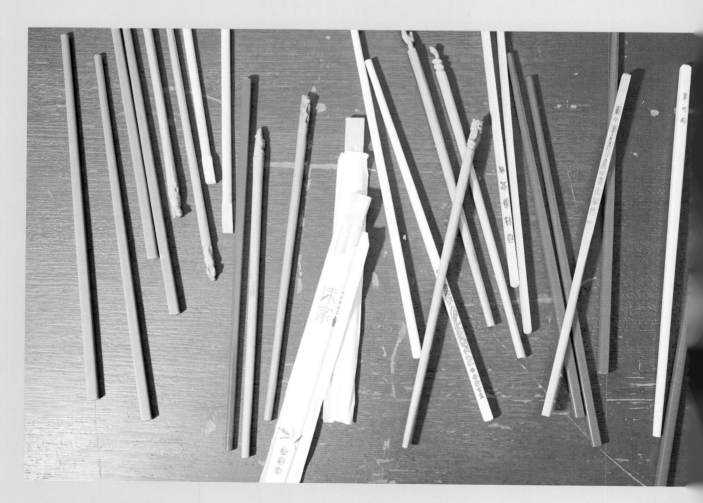

# NƯỚC MẮM

Nuoc mam dipping sauce

2 garlic cloves, finely chopped
3 bird's eye chillies, finely chopped or sliced
150 ml (5 fl oz) fish sauce
100 ml (3½ fl oz) white vinegar
140 g (5 oz) caster (superfine) sugar

**1** Combine the ingredients and 200 ml (7 fl oz) water in a bowl and stir until the sugar has dissolved.

**2** Nuoc mam can be kept in an airtight container in the fridge for up to 2 weeks.

# SATE XÃ

Lemongrass sate

This sate is great to have on hand. You can use it to marinate meats and seafood before grilling or just as a simple accompaniment to soups or as a dipping sauce. Make the full recipe, and keep anything you don't use in a sterilised sealed jar in the fridge, where it will keep for up to six months. I also like making large batches of this and giving it to friends.

6 lemongrass stalks, white part only, sliced
15 long red chillies, sliced
6 bird's eye chillies, sliced
3 brown onions, chopped
12 garlic cloves
1.5 litres (1.5 qts) vegetable oil
150 ml (5 fl oz) fish sauce

**1** In a food processor, individually blitz the lemongrass, long chillies, bird's eye chillies, onion and garlic.

**2** Place the blitzed onion in a square of muslin (cheesecloth) and squeeze out and discard any excess liquid.

**3** Heat the oil in a large saucepan over low heat to 80°C (175°F) on a kitchen thermometer. Stirring regularly throughout the whole process to avoid burning, empty the onion from the muslin into the oil and cook for 10 minutes. Add the garlic and cook for 5 minutes, then add both the chillies and cook for 20–30 minutes. Finally, add the lemongrass and fish sauce and cook for 20 minuntes or until the sate is a rich red colour.

**4** Set aside to cool completely, then spoon into a sterilised jar and seal. The sate will keep in the fridge for up to 6 months.

# MỠ HÀNH
Spring onion oil

3 spring onions (scallions), thinly sliced
pinch of salt
100 ml (3½ fl oz) vegetable oil

**1**  Place the spring onion and salt in a metal bowl.

**2**  Heat the vegetable oil in a small saucepan to 150°C (300°F) on a kitchen thermometer, then pour the oil over the spring onion. Stir and set aside to infuse until you are ready to use.

**3**  Spring onion oil should be used the same day it is made.

# BƠ
Vietnamese butter

4 egg yolks
pinch of salt
400 ml (14 fl oz) vegetable oil, plus extra
  if needed

**1**  Place the egg yolks and salt in a food processor. Blitz to combine.

**2**  With the motor running, very slowly add the oil in a thin, steady stream. The bo should become thick and firm and resemble soft butter. If the bo hasn't thickened by the time you've added all the oil, add a little more oil until it comes together.

**3**  Bo will keep in an airtight container in the fridge for 2–3 days, but I dare you to make it last that long!

# PÂTÉ

Chicken liver pate

50 ml (1¾ fl oz) vegetable oil
250 g (9 oz) chicken livers
75 g (2½ oz) onion, minced
50 g (1¾ oz) garlic, minced
2 tablespoons Cognac
50 g (1¾ oz) minced (ground) pork
75 g (2½ oz) pork fat, minced
1 egg
125 g (4½ oz) sandwich bread slices, crusts
   removed and soaked in 1 litre (34 fl oz/4 cups)
   full-cream (whole) milk

**1**   Heat 2 tablespoons of the oil in a frying pan over medium–high heat, add the chicken livers and cook for 3–5 minutes until lightly golden and cooked through. Remove from the pan and set aside.

**2**   Heat the remaining oil in the same pan, add the onion and cook for 3–5 minutes until fragrant, then add the garlic and cook for 2–3 minutes. Return the livers to the pan and lightly toss together. Carefully pour in the Cognac – the mixture will ignite so stand back – and toss the mixture until the alcohol burns off and the flames have disappeared. Remove from the pan and set aside to cool.

**3**   Combine the cooled liver mixture, minced pork, pork fat, egg and bread and milk in a large bowl and mix well. Transfer to a food processor and blitz until smooth.

**4**   Preheat the oven to 180°C (350°F). Line a 25 cm × 12 cm (10 in × 4¾ in) loaf (bar) tin with foil and pour in the pate. Cover tightly with foil.

**5**   Place the tin in a baking dish and pour enough hot water into the baking dish to come half way up the side of the loaf tin. Cover the baking dish with foil and bake for 1 hour. Check to see if the pate is set; if it's not firm, return to the oven and continue to cook until set and cooked through.

**6**   Allow the pate to cool completely at room temperature, then transfer the tin to the fridge and leave to set overnight. Remove the pate from the tin and peel away the foil. Cut the pate into slices or smaller pieces and keep in an airtight container in the fridge for 3–4 days.

# ĐÔ CHUA

Pickled carrot and daikon

1 kg (2 lb 3 oz) carrots, cut into matchsticks
300 g (10½ oz) daikon (white radish), cut into
  matchsticks

**Pickle liquid**
150 ml (5 fl oz) white vinegar
100 g (3½ oz) caster (superfine) sugar

**1** To make the pickle liquid, combine the vinegar and sugar in a bowl and add 100 ml (3½ fl oz) water. Stir until the sugar has dissolved.

**2** Rinse the daikon and carrot under warm running water for 5 minutes, then drain thoroughly and pat dry with paper towel. Transfer to a large plastic container or non-reactive bowl.

**3** Pour the pickle liquid over the vegetables and set aside in the fridge for 2 days, after which time the pickles will be ready to use.

**4** Pickled carrot and daikon will keep in the fridge for up to 2 weeks.

**Note:** The pickle liquid can also be used to pickle other ingredients, such as green papaya, kohlrabi and radish.

# HÀNH PHI

Fried shallots

300 ml (10 fl oz) vegetable oil
4 shallots, thinly sliced

**1**  Heat the vegetable oil in a small saucepan to 170°C (340°F) on a kitchen thermometer.

**2**  Place the shallot in the oil and cook, stirring continuously to break up the shallot, for 7–8 minutes until golden brown.

**3**  Using a slotted spoon, remove the shallot from the oil and drain on a plate lined with paper towel. Using two forks, quickly separate and loosen the shallot – if it stays in a clump it will burn in the residual heat.

**4**  Fried shallots will keep in an airtight container for 2–3 days.

**MAKES 250 ml (8½ fl oz)**

# DÂU TOỎ

Garlic oil

200 ml (7 fl oz) vegetable oil
10 garlic cloves, minced

**1**  Heat the vegetable oil in a small saucepan to 70°C (160°F) on a kitchen thermometer.

**2**  Place the garlic in the oil and cook, stirring continuously to break up the garlic, for 5 minutes until light golden brown. Remove from the heat and set aside cool.

**3**  The garlic oil will keep in an airtight container in the fridge for up to 4 days.

# RUỐC TÔM

*Prawn floss*

100 g (3½ oz) dried shrimp

**1**  Rehydrate the shrimp in cold water for 3 hours or, preferably, overnight. Drain and pat dry with paper towel.

**2**  Put the shrimp in a food processor and blitz to a fine floss.

**3**  Heat a large frying pan over low heat, add the shrimp and cook, stirring continuously, for 10 minutes or until dry.

**4**  Store in an airtight container in the pantry for up to 1 week.

# ĐẬU PHỘNG RANG

*Roasted peanuts*

100 g (3½ oz) raw peanuts (without skins)

**1**  Preheat the oven to 180°C (350°F).

**2**  Place the peanuts on a baking tray and roast, checking them frequently to ensure they don't burn, for 10–15 minutes until golden brown.

**3**  Allow to cool, then lightly crush.

**4**  The crushed peanuts will keep in an airtight container in the pantry for 1–2 weeks.

# NƯỚC MẮM ỚT XANH

Green chilli dipping sauce

**Makes 300 ml (10 fl oz)**

2 long green chillies, roughly chopped

2 garlic cloves, roughly chopped

3 tablespoons caster (superfine) sugar, plus extra if needed

2 tablespoons freshly squeezed lime juice, plus extra if needed

3 tablespoons fish sauce, plus extra if needed

**1** Place all the ingredients in a blender and blend to a smooth sauce.

**2** Check the seasoning – it should be sweet, sour, salty and spicy – and adjust with a little more sugar, lime juice or fish sauce if necessary.

**3** Store in an airtight container in the fridge for 2–3 days.

# DẦU HẠT ĐIỀU

Annatto oil

**MAKES 200 ml (7 fl oz)**

200 ml (7 fl oz) vegetable oil

1 teaspoon annatto seeds

**1** Heat the vegetable oil in a small saucepan to 70°C (160°F) on a kitchen thermometer.

**2** Place the annatto seeds in the oil and cook for 5 minutes until the oil turns a vibrant orange.

**3** Remove from the heat, strain through a fine mesh sieve and set aside to cool. Discard the seeds.

**4** The oil will keep in an airtight container in the fridge for 2–3 days.

# MẮM NÊM

Mam nem dressing

20 g (¾ oz) ginger
20 g (¾ oz) garlic
20 g (¾ oz) long red chillies
350 g (12½ oz) pineapple, peeled, cored
  and roughly chopped
100 ml (3½ fl oz) coconut water
150 ml (5 fl oz) mam nem (anchovy sauce)
150 ml (5 fl oz) lemonade

**1** Place the ginger, garlic, chilli and pineapple in a blender and blend to a rough paste. Transfer to a saucepan, add the remaining ingredients and place over medium heat. Simmer the sauce for 20–30 minutes until slightly thickened and fragrant.

**2** Set aside until completely cool, then transfer to an airtight container and keep in the fridge for 2–3 days.

ACKNOWLEDGEMENTS

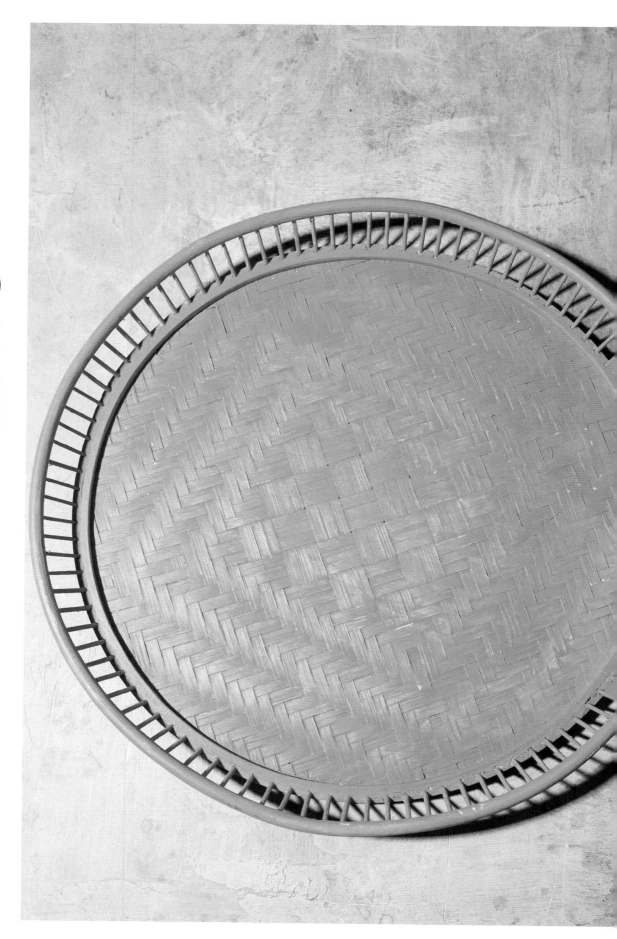

This book has been a labour of love, and I could not have done it alone.

I would like to thank my wife, Eliza, for her love and support. I couldn't do any of this without you. You are my rock and the best mother our boy could ever hope for. Being the partner of a chef is a tough gig!

I'd like to thank my parents, who remain my harshest critics and culinary inspiration. I hope you enjoy reading and cooking from this book.

My good friend and general manager, Olivia Hardie, thank you for your ever-enduring patience and support. Without your hard work this book would not have come to life.

I'd like to recognise my kitchen and front-of-house team at Pho Nom and Annam. Your diligence, enthusiasm and excitement in bringing my vision for Vietnamese food to life for our guests is forever valued.

To my legendary friends – Suzanne Roney, Rani Doyle, Chloe Boulton, Simone Ardern, Chris Donnellan and Kate Whalen – thank you for always being willing taste-testers, hand-holders and shoulders to cry on.

Thank you to Paul McNally, publisher of Smith Street Books, who gave me the opportunity to write my first book on a subject that is dear to me; and to Lucy Heaver, who has edited the book and suffered through my delays with elegance and grace.

To photographer Chris Middleton and stylist Deb Kaloper, thank you for capturing my vision and the essence of super-fresh Vietnamese street food.

Finally, this book is dedicated to my son, Harry. I can't wait to share my passion for Vietnamese food with you and cook these recipes together as you grow.

Jerry Mai is a Vietnamese–Australian chef living and working in Melbourne, Australia. She has spent 20 years working in some of Melbourne's greatest kitchen institutions including Longrain, Gingerboy and Seamstress.

In 2009, Jerry set off to London to work in Michelin-starred restaurants, starting at Nahm, where she excelled under the watchful eye of David Thompson, before moving onto Zuma, the acclaimed Japanese restaurant frequented and loved by London rockstars. Her experiences overseas refined her skills and allowed Jerry to bring her own signature style back to Melbourne and apply it to the Vietnamese food she so dearly loves, in a manner never before seen in Australia.

Jerry owns and runs two restaurants offering different Vietnamese food experiences – the cool, casual street-food of Pho Nom, and Annam, Jerry's pimped-up Vietnamese restaurant showcasing her mother's recipes, all intertwined with her own unique food experiences.

This is her first cookbook.

ABOUT THE
AUTHOR

# A

anchovies 37
anchovy sauce 15
Annatto oil 214
**apples**
    Beef cooked on a hotplate 106
    Salmon and apple rice paper
      rolls 49

# B

*bạc hà* 17
**banana blossom** 15
    Banana blossom and crispy tofu
      salad 122
    banana blossom salad 138
banana, Coconut fried 195
*Bánh bèo* 35
*Bánh canh cua* 145
*Bánh cuốn của* 29
*Bánh mì heo quay* 64
*Bánh mì ốp la* 67
*Bánh mì xíu mại* 70
*Bánh tằm bì* 112
*Bánh tôm* 32
*bánh tráng* 16, 40
*Bánh tráng nướng* 57
*Bánh tráng trộn* 58
*Bánh xèo* 26
*bắp chuối* 15
*Bắp nướng phô mai* 90
**beans**
    Three colour che 186
    Waterfern cakes 35
**beef**
    Beef cooked on a hotplate 106
    Beef pho 153
    broth 138, 153
    Grilled beef wrapped in betel leaf 79
    *Lẩu* 148
    Rare beef salad 128
    Saigon breakfast hotplate 72
    Spicy beef noodle soup 138
Beef cooked on a hotplate 106
Beef pho 153
beer 96
betel leaf 17
*Bơ* 207
*Bò lá lốt* 79
*Bò né Saigon* 72
*Bò nướng vỉ* 106
*bột gạo* 16
Braised chicken in ginger 166
Braised meatball banh mi 70
Broken rice with pork chop 165

broths 134, 137, 138, 142, 145, 146, 153,
    154, 158
*bún* 16
*Bún bò huế* 138
*Bún chả Hanoi* 80
Bún riêu 134
*Bún thịt nướng* 87
Butter 207

# C

*Cà chua nhồi thịt* 171
*Cá nướng cuốn bánh tráng* 82
*Cà phê caramel* 196
*Cà phê sữa đá* 198
*Cà phê trứng* 199
**cabbage**
    broth 158
    Mushroom and tofu pho 158
    Poached chicken slaw 125
    slaw 125
**calamari**
    Chilli salt calamari 88
    Five-spice calamari 100
    *Lẩu* 148
    Phnom Penh noodle soup 137
*cánh hồi* 16
*Canh tôm bị đau* 176
capsicum: Five-spice calamari 100
caramel, salted 189
Caramelised pork belly 168
**carrots**
    Beef cooked on a hotplate 106
    Braised meatball banh mi 70
    Broken rice with pork chop 165
    broth 158
    Chargrilled pork patties with herbs
      and noodles 80
    Fried egg banh mi 67
    Grilled fish in rice paper 82
    Hoi An chicken rice 179
    Jellyfish and duck salad 120
    Mushroom and tofu pho 158
    Noodles with shredded pork and
      coconut dressing 112
    Pickled carrot and daikon 209
    pickles 80
    Poached chicken slaw 125
    Prawn and pomelo salad 114
    Prawn and pork salad with green
      papaya 119
    Rare beef salad 128
    Roast pork belly banh mi 64
    slaw 125
cassia bark 15
ceviche dressing 128
*chả giò cua và thịt heo* 52

*Cháo gà* 146
Chargrilled pork patties with herbs
    and noodles 80
*Chè ba màu* 186
*Chè thái* 184
cheese: Grilled sweet corn with Laughing
    Cow cheese 90
*Chem chép hấp bia và là quê* 98
**chicken**
    Braised chicken in ginger 166
    broth 134, 137, 142, 145, 154
    chicken broth 146
    Chicken congee 146
    Chicken liver pate 208
    Chicken pho 154
    Crab and thick rice noodles 145
    Crab noodle soup 134
    Hoi An chicken rice 179
    *Lẩu* 148
    Phnom Penh noodle soup 137
    Poached chicken slaw 125
    Prawn dumplings with egg
      noodles 142
chicken broth 146
Chicken congee 146
Chicken liver pate 208
Chicken pho 154
chilli salt 88
Chilli salt calamari 88
chilli sate 138
*Chuối chiên dừa* 195
citrus–soy dressing 122
*cổ phiếu chính* 15
**coconut**
    Coconut fried banana 195
    Three colour che 186
    Vietnamese fruit cocktail 184
coconut cream 112
Coconut fried banana 195
**coffee**
    Coffee caramel 196
    Egg coffee 199
    Frozen yoghurt coffee 199
    Vietnamese iced coffee 198
Coffee caramel 196
*Cơm gà hội an* 179
*Cơm tấm* 165
congee, Chicken 146
corn: Grilled sweet corn with Laughing
    Cow cheese 90
**crab**
    Crab and pork spring rolls 52
    Crab and thick rice noodles 145
    Crab in silken rice noodle rolls 29
    crab mix 145
    crab mousse 134
    Crab noodle soup 134
    *Lẩu* 148
    Steamed crab with green chilli
      dipping sauce 103

Crab and pork spring rolls 52
Crab and thick rice noodles 145
Crab in silken rice noodle rolls 29
crab mix 145
crab mousse 134
Crab noodle soup 134
cream, coconut 112
Crispy Vietnamese pancakes 26
*Cua hấp chấm nước mắm ớt xanh* 103
**cucumber**
    Banana blossom and crispy tofu
        salad 122
    Braised meatball banh mi 70
    Broken rice with pork chop 165
    Fried egg banh mi 67
    Grilled fish in rice paper 82
    Grilled pork and vermicelli
        noodle salad 87
    Jellyfish and duck salad 120
    Noodles with shredded pork and
        coconut dressing 112
    Prawn and pomelo salad 114
    Rare beef salad 128
    Roast pork belly banh mi 64
    Saigon breakfast hotplate 72
**cumquat**
    cumquat chilli salt 98
    Steamed crab with green chilli
        dipping sauce 103
cumquat chilli salt 98

# D

**daikon**
    Beef cooked on a hotplate 106
    Braised meatball banh mi 70
    Broken rice with pork chop 165
    broth 137, 142
    Fried egg banh mi 67
    Grilled fish in rice paper 82
    Hoi An chicken rice 179
    Jellyfish and duck salad 120
    Noodles with shredded pork and
        coconut dressing 112
    Phnom Penh noodle soup 137
    Pickled carrot and daikon 209
    Poached chicken slaw 125
    Prawn and pomelo salad 114
    Prawn and pork salad with green
        papaya 119
    Prawn dumplings with egg
        noodles 142
    Rare beef salad 128
    Roast pork belly banh mi 64
    slaw 125
*Dầu hạt điều* 214
*Đậu phộng rang* 213

*Dâu tơơ* 212
Deep-fried ice cream with
    salted caramel 189
*Dẹp nướng mỡ hành* 93
dipping sauce 148
*Đồ chua* 209
**dressings**
    citrus–soy dressing 122
    ceviche dressing 128
    galangal dressing 120
    Mam nem dressing 215
    nuoc mam dressing 114, 119
    soy and shallot dressing 58
*đu đủ xanh* 15
duck: Jellyfish and duck salad 120

# E

Egg coffee 199
**eggs**
    Broken rice with pork chop 165
    Butter 207
    Caramelised pork belly 168
    Coffee caramel 196
    Fried egg banh mi 67
    Grilled rice paper 57
    Rice paper salad with shrimp 58
    Saigon breakfast hotplate 72
elephant ear stalk 17

# F

**fish** 37
    fish sauce 15, 37
    Grilled fish in rice paper 82
    *Lẩu* 148
    *see also* salmon, seafood
fish sauce 15, 37
Fish sauce for dipping 206
Five-spice calamari 100
Fried egg banh mi 67
Fried garlic oil 212
Fried green rice prawn rice paper
    rolls 46
Fried shallots 212
fritters, School prawn and sweet
    potato 32
Frozen yoghurt coffee 199
fruit cocktail, Vietnamese 184

# G

*Gà xào gừng* 166
galangal dressing 120
glass noodles 15
*Gỏi bắp chuối tàu hủ chiên* 122
*Gỏi bò tái chanh* 128
*Gỏi cuốn cá hồi* 49
*Gỏi cuốn tôm chiên cốm dẹp xanh* 46
*Gỏi cuốn tôm hẻo* 42
*Gỏi đu đủ tôm thịt* 119
*Gỏi gà* 125
*Gỏi sứa thịt vịt* 120
*Gỏi tôm bưởi* 114
Green chilli dipping sauce 214
green mango *see* mango
green papaya *see* papaya
Grilled beef wrapped in betel leaf 79
Grilled fish in rice paper 82
Grilled pork and vermicelli noodle
    salad 87
Grilled rice paper 57
Grilled scallops 93
Grilled sweet corn with Laughing Cow
    cheese 90

# H

*Hành phi* 212
Hanoi spring rolls 50
herbs 17
Hoi An chicken rice 179
hoi sin dipping sauce 42
hoi sin sauce 15
Hotpot 148
*Hủ tiếu nam vang* 137
*húng lủi* 17

# I

ice cream, Deep-fried, with salted
    caramel 189

# J

Jellyfish and duck salad 120

# K

*Kem chiên* 189
kitchen equipment 17

# L

*lá lốt* 17
*Lẩu* 148
leeks: Crab in silken rice noodle rolls 29
Lemongrass sate 206

# M

*mắm nêm* 15
Mam nem dressing 215
*mắm ruốc* 16
**mango** 15
    Rice paper salad with shrimp 58
marinades 80, 87, 165
master stock 15
mayonnaise, wasabi 49
meatballs 70
Melon and prawn soup 176
*Mì sủi cảo* 142
*mì trứng* 16
*miến* 15
mint 17
*Mỡ hành* 207
mock pomegranate seeds 184
**morning glory** 16
    banana blossom salad 138
    Crab noodle soup 134
    *Lẩu* 148
    Stir-fried morning glory 174
*Mực nướng muối ớt* 88
*Mực rang muối* 100
**mushroom**
    Broken rice with pork chop 165
    Crab and pork spring rolls 52
    Hanoi spring rolls 50
    *Lẩu* 148
    Mushroom and tofu pho 158
    pork loaf 165
    Prawn dumplings with egg
      noodles 142
    sui cao 142
Mushroom and tofu pho 158
Mussels in Thai basil Bia Hanoi 98

# N

*Nem rán* 50
*ngò gai* 17
*ngò om* 17
**noodles**
    Grilled pork and vermicelli noodle
      salad 87
    Beef cooked on a hotplate 106
    Beef pho 153
    Chargrilled pork patties with herbs
      and noodles 80
    Chicken pho 154
    Crab and thick rice noodles 145
    Crab noodle soup 134
    Fried green rice prawn rice paper
      rolls 46
    glass noodles 15
    Grilled fish in rice paper 82
    Hanoi spring rolls 50
    *Lẩu* 148
    Mushroom and tofu pho 158
    Noodles with shredded pork and
      coconut dressing 112
    Phnom Penh noodle soup 137
    Pork and prawn rice paper rolls 42
    pork loaf 165
    Pork-stuffed tomatoes with dill 171
    Prawn dumplings with egg
      noodles 142
    rice noodles 16
    Spicy beef noodle soup 138
    thin egg noodles 16
Noodles with shredded pork and coconut
   dressing 112
*nước mắm* 15, 37
*Nước mắm* 206
nuoc mam dressing 114, 119
Nuoc mam dipping sauce 206
*Nước mắm ớt xanh* 214

# O

**oils**
    Annatto oil 214
    Fried garlic oil 212
    Spring onion oil 207
oyster sauce 16

# P

**pancakes**
    Crispy vietnamese pancakes 26
    Savoury mini coconut pancakes 24
pandan jelly 186
pantry staples 15–17
**papaya** 15
    Chargrilled pork patties with herbs
      and noodles 80
    Hoi An chicken rice 179
    pickles 80
    Prawn and pork salad with
      green papaya 119
    salad 179
*Pâté* 208
pate, Chicken liver 208
**peanuts**
    Banana blossom and crispy
      tofu salad 122
    Grilled fish in rice paper 82
    Grilled pork and vermicelli noodle
      salad 87
    Grilled scallops 93
    Prawn and pork salad with
      green papaya 119
    Rare beef salad 128
    Rice paper salad with shrimp 58
    Roasted peanuts 213
Phnom Penh noodle soup 137
**pho** 132
    Beef pho 153
    Chicken pho 154
    how to eat 151
    Mushroom and tofu pho 158
*Phở bò* 153
*Phở chay* 158
*Phở gà* 154
pickle liquid 209
Pickled carrot and daikon 209
pickles 80
**pineapple**
    Beef cooked on a hotplate 106
    broth 138
    Grilled fish in rice paper 82
    Mam nem dressing 215
    Spicy beef noodle soup 138
Poached chicken slaw 125
pomegranate seeds, mock 184
pomelo: Prawn and pomelo salad 114
**pork**
    Braised meatball banh mi 70
    Broken rice with pork chop 165
    broth 134, 137, 138, 145
    Caramelised pork belly 168
    Chargrilled pork patties with herbs
      and noodles 80
    Chicken liver pate 208
    Crab and pork spring rolls 52
    Crab and thick rice noodles 145
    Crab noodle soup 134
    Crispy vietnamese pancakes 26
    Grilled beef wrapped in betel leaf 79

Grilled pork and vermicelli noodle salad 87
Grilled sweet corn with Laughing Cow cheese 90
Hanoi spring rolls 50
meatballs 70
Noodles with shredded pork and coconut dressing 112
Phnom Penh noodle soup 137
Pork and prawn rice paper rolls 42
pork loaf 165
Pork-stuffed tomatoes with dill 171
Prawn and pork salad with green papaya 119
Prawn dumplings with egg noodles 142
Roast pork belly banh mi 64
shredded pork 112
Spicy beef noodle soup 138
Waterfern cakes 35
Pork and prawn rice paper rolls 42
pork belly 64
pork loaf 165
Pork-stuffed tomatoes with dill 171
Prawn and pomelo salad 114
Prawn and pork salad with green papaya 119
Prawn dumplings with egg noodles 142
Prawn floss 213
**prawns**
Crispy Vietnamese pancakes 26
Fried green rice prawn rice paper rolls 46
*Lẩu* 148
Melon and prawn soup 176
Phnom Penh noodle soup 137
Pork and prawn rice paper rolls 42
Prawn and pomelo salad 114
Prawn and pork salad with green papaya 119
Prawn dumplings with egg noodles 142
Prawn floss 213
Savoury mini coconut pancakes 24
School prawn and sweet potato fritters 32
sui cao 142
Waterfern cakes 35

**Q**

quail eggs *see* eggs
*quế* 15

**R**

Rare beef salad 128
*rau muống* 16
*Rau muống xào tương* 174
*rau quế* 17
*rau răm* 17
**rice** 40
Braised chicken in ginger 166
Broken rice with pork chop 165
Caramelised pork belly 168
Chicken congee 146
Fried green rice prawn rice paper rolls 46
Hoi An chicken rice 179
Noodles with shredded pork and coconut dressing 112
Pork-stuffed tomatoes with dill 171
Yoghurt with black sticky rice 190
rice flour 16
rice noodles 16
rice paddy herb 17
rice paper 16, 40
Rice paper salad with shrimp 58
Roast pork belly banh mi 64
Roasted peanuts 213
**rolls**
Crab and pork spring rolls 52
Crab in silken rice noodle rolls 29
Fried green rice prawn rice paper rolls 46
Hanoi spring rolls 50
Pork and prawn rice paper rolls 42
Salmon and apple rice paper rolls 49
*Ruốc tôm* 213

**S**

Saigon breakfast hotplate 72
**salads** 110, 134, 179
Banana blossom and crispy tofu salad 122
Grilled pork and vermicelli noodle salad 87
Jellyfish and duck salad 120
Noodles with shredded pork and coconut dressing 112
Poached chicken slaw 125
Prawn and pomelo salad 114
Prawn and pork salad with green papaya 119
Rare beef salad 128
Rice paper salad with shrimp 58
Salmon and apple rice paper rolls 49

**salt**
chilli salt 88
cumquat chilli salt 98
salted caramel 189
*Sate xã* 206
sate, Lemongrass 206
**sauces** 70
anchovy sauce 15
fish sauce 15
Green chilli dipping sauce 214
hoi sin dipping sauce 42
hoi sin sauce 15
Lemongrass sate 206
Mam nem dressing 215
Nuoc mam dipping sauce 206
oyster sauce 16
shrimp sauce 16
wasabi mayonnaise 49
sausages: Grilled sweet corn with Laughing Cow cheese 90
Savoury mini coconut pancakes 24
sawtooth coriander 17
scallops, Grilled 93
School prawn and sweet potato fritters 32
**seafood**
Grilled scallops 93
Jellyfish and duck salad 120
*see also* calamari, crab, fish, prawns, scallops, shrimp
shallots, Fried 212
shiso 17
shredded pork 112
**shrimp**
crab mousse 134
Crab noodle soup 134
Grilled rice paper 57
Phnom Penh noodle soup 137
Prawn floss 213
Rice paper salad with shrimp 58
shrimp sauce 16
slaw 125
slaw, Poached chicken 125
*sốt hàu* 16
*sốt tương ngọt* 15
**soups**
Crab noodle soup 134
Hotpot 148
Melon and prawn soup 176
Phnom Penh noodle soup 137
Spicy beef noodle soup 138
*see also* pho
soy and shallot dressing 58
Spicy beef noodle soup 138
Spring onion oil 207
spring rolls, Crab and pork 52
spring rolls, Hanoi 50
**squid**
broth 137
Phnom Penh noodle soup 137

star anise 16
Steamed crab with green chilli dipping
    sauce 103
Stir-fried morning glory 174
stock, master 15
*Sửa chữa* 192
*Sửa chua cà phê* 199
*Sửa chua nếp cẩm* 190
sui cao 142
sweet potato: School prawn and sweet
    potato fritters 32

Crab noodle soup 134
Pork-stuffed tomatoes with dill 171
Saigon breakfast hotplate 72
sauce 70

# T

Thai basil 17
thin egg noodles 16
*Thịt kho* 168
Three colour che 186
*tía tô* 17
**tofu**
    Banana blossom and crispy tofu
      salad 122
    Crab noodle soup 134
    Mushroom and tofu pho 158
**tomatoes**
    Broken rice with pork chop 165

# V

Vietnamese fruit cocktail 184
Vietnamese iced coffee 198
Vietnamese mint 17
Vietnamese Yoghurt 192

# W

wasabi mayonnaise 49
Waterfern cakes 35

# X

xoài xanh 15

# Y

Yoghurt with black sticky rice 190
yoghurt, Vietnamese 192

Published in 2019 by Smith Street Books
Melbourne | Australia
smithstreetbooks.com

ISBN: 978-1-925811-04-9 (Hardcase)
ISBN: 978-1-925811-12-4 (Flexicase)

The moral right of the author has been asserted.
CIP data is available from the National Library of Australia.

Publisher: Paul McNally
Senior editor: Lucy Heaver, Tusk studio
Designer: Evi O Studio | Evi O
Photographer: Chris Middleton
Stylist: Deb Kaloper
Food preparation: Jerry Mai
Printed & bound in China by C&C Offset Printing Co., Ltd.

Book 90
10 9 8 7 6 5 4 3 2 1